IMAGES
of America

HEBRON

This intriguing photograph is from the Foote family collection. It depicts Edward Foote's gentleness with a newborn deer, a trait for which he was well known—notice the intensity in his face. It didn't matter if it was a calf, a deer, or any other species of young animal—with lots of patience, Ed taught them to drink to survive.

IMAGES
of America

HEBRON

Hebron Historical Society

ARCADIA
PUBLISHING

Published by Arcadia Publishing
Charleston, South Carolina

Library of Congress Catalog Card Number: 2004106823

For all general information, contact Arcadia Publishing:
Telephone 843-853-2070
Fax 843-853-0044
E-mail sales@arcadiapublishing.com
For customer service and orders:
Toll-Free 1-888-313-2665

Visit us on the Internet at www.arcadiapublishing.com

On the cover: The cover depicts P. W. Turner's silk mill No. 1 in 1905. Notice the running water needed for operation. In 1947, Rev. George Milne delivered an historical sermon at Hope Valley Church in which he reminded attendees to consider the mills' importance in Amston history. The silk mills are long gone, and this is one of the few surviving photographs of the men and women who worked in them.

Raphael Kassman is shown far left, and in the center of this 1943 photograph from the Jones-Porter collection, Sherm Miner sits in his usual chair in front of Alma Porter's store and post office. Children gather to buy ice cream. Few today remember the gas pumps in front of the store. However, the real scene-stealer is Tiny, Alma and Clarence Porter's dog, doing what comes naturally.

CONTENTS

ACKNOWLEDGMENTS

This is the first book on Hebron history since John Sibun's *Our Town's Heritage 1708–1958: Hebron, Connecticut*, published in 1975. There are many people to thank for their participation in this, a genuine community effort. The following people have contributed numerous photographs, diaries, and documents from their private collections, many of which have never been viewed by the public: Paul and Carla Pomprowicz, Merle Jones Porter, Elizabeth Hutchinson (Betsy) Foote Osborn, Mary Ann Foote, Winthrop Hilding, Alberta Hilding, Marie Smith Billard, Donald Robinson, Margaret Keefe Ely, Dorothy Brehant Taggart, Betty Jones Ous, Henry and Mary Jones, Lloyd Gray, Vivian Lajoie Horton, Ned and Renee Ellis, Alan and Denise Hills, Bruce and Roberta Porter DeGray, Jean Raymond, Laura Jones Mund, Joan Pagach Toomey, Joan Landon, Grace Rathbun Grubert, Robert Jones, Stanley and Natalie Attardo Walas, Douglas and Mary Porter, Wallace P. Clebowicz, and Robert Norton Warner. This book could not have been completed without the assistance and input of Betsy Foote Osborn in the final days before deadline. Milton Porter and Ronald Parkyn, commander of the Hebron VFW, provided detailed information about Hebron residents who served in the two world wars.

There are so many wonderful poets in our Hebron family. While Susan Bingham Pendleton is the most famous, Edward Ashley Smith also wrote volumes of poetry, even as he worked daily on his farm. Dorothy Brehant Taggart is a prolific and published poet, as well. But it is Lucille "Lulu" Porter Jones's poem "Don't Worry Mom," in her *Reflections*, that gives us all pause. She had just learned that her son, Carlton Porter Jones, had been killed in action in 1944.

> "Don't worry Mom, I'll hurry back
> as soon as this war is won.
> I'll finish all the things and such
> that I had just begun.
> We'll take that trip we talked about
> there's lots of things to see.
> Don't worry Mom, I'll be right back"
> Is what he said to me.
>
> The war is not yet over
> The victory not yet won.
> But he will never finish
> the things he'd just begun.
> He told me not to worry
> and he asked me not to cry
> "Don't worry Mom," is what he said.
> And then he said Goodbye.

At Alice Elizabeth Hills Foote's funeral, Rev. George Milne thanked God "for her gift of living in the present, and of bringing to a new age the wisdom and insights and values of an elder day." This book is dedicated to all of those, young and old, who—for almost 300 years—have worked hard to bring solid values of love of God, love of country, and love of community into the Hebron we have gratefully inherited in the 21st century.

—Donna J. McCalla, President, Hebron Historical Society, 2004

INTRODUCTION

Like so much territory on which Connecticut towns were founded, the American Indians originally owned Hebron's land. However, unlike most of the towns in Connecticut, the land in Hebron was not obtained by seizure or conquest. Rather, it was obtained in the form of a legacy, drawn up by Joshua. In February 1676, Joshua—or Attawanhood as he was named by his father, Uncas, Great Sachem of the Mohegan tribe—signed over the land to Edward Shipman, William Lord, and others of the Old Saybrook Legatees. Twenty-eight years passed before any white men settled on the land.

William Shipman (son of Edward) and Timothy Phelps arrived from Windsor in 1704. The first spot to be named in the area was Prophet's Rock. It was a place that afforded protection from the elements to both travelers and animals. It was near Prophet's Rock that the first homes were built and fields cleared; it became the first center of town. Hebron was formally incorporated in 1708.

By act of the General Assembly in October 1716, the First Congregational Church was organized. John Bliss conducted services in private homes and in a barn that was located just behind the present First Congregational Church. At that time, the town and church were one, but all was not blissful. Religious differences between congregation members living on the north side of town and those on the south side tore Hebron apart physically and spiritually. Bliss and 20 families split off and built the first St. Peter's Episcopal Church in 1734 near Slocum Road. That original church is no longer existent; the current St. Peter's on Church Street was built in 1826. The Gilead Congregational Church was built in 1838. As the town grew, so did the number, size, and location of its churches.

When the French and Indian War ended in 1758, the people of Hebron wanted to demonstrate their loyalty to the king. To that end, the local blacksmith hollowed out a huge log to make a cannon of 120-pound caliber—also known as a pump. Abigail Pomeroy, the wife of the minister of the First Congregational Church, actually fired the cannon. It would be fired just that one time, because the cannon blew itself apart in the process. It was exactly the sort of blast and excitement that the participants were looking for. The demonstration was so well publicized that it eventually came to the attention of King George II. Wishing to make the proper acknowledgment, he decided to present the townspeople of Hebron a brass cannon as a gift. The cannon never arrived, however, and was reported to have been lost at sea. The town was nicknamed "Pump Town" in memory of that event. But whoever designed the town logo obviously hadn't heard the legend; the logo erroneously depicts a hand-driven water pump, not the old log cannon.

Hebron's big fire of 1882 started on April 17, on a very windy day, at 2:30 in the afternoon. The students at the school across the Green were the first to see the glow on the roof of the Leonard's store, which sat right next to the Congregational church. Chimney sparks either from the store itself or from the nearby Hendee house started the fire. It was reported that the church burned to the ground in 20 minutes. The blaze destroyed the store and the church on the west and north of the Green. It moved eastward, and destroyed every structure except a house and harness shop that were set back from the Green. The fire also damaged the town hall, and burned the Norton house and schoolhouse to the ground. The church was promptly rebuilt, and it was dedicated on May 5, 1883.

There were various library associations in the late 1800s. In 1888, the General Assembly of the State of Connecticut incorporated the Hebron Literary Society, and Ida Porter Douglas (wife of Dr. Charles Douglas) became the moving spirit in a project to secure and construct a library building. The Hebron Public Library, built next to the town hall, was formally dedicated on June 21, 1898. The library operated independently, thanks largely to membership fees, strong annual contributions, and a $160,000 endowment from Dr. Charles Douglas, who upon his death in 1947, included the caveat that the building be renamed the Douglas Library in honor of his wife, Ida.

Change came to Hebron in the 20th century, just as it did to all American towns. With the opening of the Turnerville (Amston) rail depot—also called the Airline—busy travelers between Boston and New York brought an economic boom, especially to the southern part of the town. Inns, boarding rooms, little general stores, and other cottage industries flourished alongside the large mills and manufacturing plants. There were great expectations of future success in most of these ventures, but the reality was that the business owners were borrowing money—a lot of money—to begin their enterprises. One of those who borrowed heavily was Charles Ams, the creator of the Ams-Sterling Roadster. With those borrowed funds Ams bought so much of the Turner land and water rights that the town name of Turnerville was changed to Amston. But Ams's Sterling Automobile Company, which opened in late 1917 to a great flourish of publicity, went out of business less than two years later. The bankruptcy documents noted that only about $1,700 in assets remained by November 1919, which was not enough money to pay off the creditors, much less the investors who had purchased 100,000 shares of Sterling stock. P. W. Turner, owner of the silk mill and most of the water rights in the area (including the lake), "remembered" to repay portions of his debts (see page 61), but his business also struggled and failed to survive the Great Depression.

Just as the trains had stimulated growth in Hebron in the late 1800s and early 1900s, new transportation means and technology eroded it. More paved roads and highways were put in, and trucking replaced trains as the preferred mode of transportation. The Depression ultimately sealed the fate of many of the early Hebron business ventures. Technological changes in agriculture affected the area's farms; today, there are only a handful of the original farmlands left.

Hebron is but one attempt to capture just some of these moments in time, moments in Hebron's history.

—Wallace P. Clebowicz, author of *Hebron, CT: Then and Now*, and Donna J. McCalla

One

THE FACES

This famous image of Connecticut governor John Peters, who served from 1831 to 1832, is still owned by a Hebron resident. It depicts St. Peter's Episcopal Church in the background. Born in Hebron in 1772, Peters started his career as a doctor and practiced medicine in his hometown until he entered politics in 1810. Later in life, Governor Peters became president of the Connecticut State Medical Society and vice president of the Connecticut Historical Society. He never married.

Julius Hills and his wife, Elizabeth Mitchell Hills, are pictured c. 1890. They owned the farmland across from what is now Blackledge Country Club, on West Street. One interesting thing about Mr. and Mrs. Hills is that their daughters (and other female Hills descendants) married into other local farming families. There are few longtime residents who can't find a Hills woman in their genealogy.

This is a photograph of George C. Tennant Sr. and his children. From left to right are the following: (first row) Chester, Annie, George Sr., and Louis; (second row) Harry, George Jr., Randall, Charles, and Jared. The photograph was taken c. 1920 at the Tennant homestead on Millstream Road. Harry Tennant was a successful photographer who owned stores in both Hebron and East Hampton.

Generations of Porters gathered in 1987 in honor of Ethel Hills Porter's 90th birthday. The youngest in attendance, eight-month-old Kara Bolles, sits in Ethel's lap (front and center). Douglas and Mary Porter, well-known Hebron dairy farmers, stand just left of center in the photograph.

Carroll William Hutchinson and his sister Annie Lovina, pictured here in 1889, were the children of Alfred and Lovina Holbrook Hutchinson. Annie's aunt Ellen Elizabeth Holbrook made her gray dress trimmed with red velvet. Annie wrote of childhood memories in her *In Gilead*: "When the toil of the day is over, and the weary sigh for rest, There is peace on Gilead's hilltop as the sun sets in the west."

Ellen Brown inherited land from her family, property which dated back to the original settlement of Hebron that was purchased from Joshua Sachem's allotment to the new settlers. In 1895, she sold 102 acres to her cousin, Wilbur Newton Hills, who then began a serious dairy operation. Ellen moved to Andover, but the Brown and the Hills families remained close. The Hills's dairy operation is still thriving today.

Frederick John Brehant married Ethel May Rogers on July 17, 1921. He was not yet an American citizen, having emigrated from Guernsey, England, when he was 18 years old. Brehant was a blacksmith and carpenter; Rogers was a teacher at Lyman's Viaduct. The couple met at Hebron Congregational Church. A very young Mervin Little went to Holbrook's Pond to gather the pond lilies for Ethel's wedding bouquet, seen here.

Melissa Hills Jones is shown here in 1910 with her son Ben (center), Ben's son Elmer, and Elmer's young son Clarence. In 1856 Melissa married Flavel Jones, her teacher, just before her 16th birthday. Flavel taught in the East Hampton school district for 31 years. He was also a stonemason and helped build the Tolland jail. Melissa ran the couple's small dairy operation. The photograph is from the Robert Jones collection.

Arguably one of the most beautiful women born in Hebron, Annie Tennant, the only daughter of George C. Tennant Sr., is shown here in the 1890s. She ultimately married Leon Rathbone, and they lived on Church Street. Some of the Rathbone family, who emigrated from England, changed the spelling of the name to either Rathbun or Rathburn.

Alice Elizabeth Hills and Edward Erastus Foote married in 1890; these are their engagement pictures. The following year the Footes purchased the Strickland farm in Gilead and began their careers as dairy farmers. Both were members of the Gilead Congregational Church. Alice was especially famous for her braided rugs, quilts, and doughnuts. She died in her 112th year and was the oldest resident of Connecticut at the time of her passing. She, Edward, and their three children are buried in the Gilead Cemetery.

Who doesn't love a parade? It is Memorial Day, May 30, 1922. The flag is flying, the vehicles are lined up, the family is dressed up, and three generations of Hutchinsons and Footes have gathered at the old homestead in Gilead. The photographer's attention is centered on the unregistered, energy-conserving vehicle (the horse and buggy) driven by Alfred W. and Lovina (Holbrook) Hutchinson, who are celebrating their golden wedding anniversary.

Family members are gathered in 1922 in Gilead to celebrate the Hutchinsons' 50th wedding anniversary. From left to right are the following: (first row) Mildred Hutchinson, Marjorie Foote, Everett Hutchinson, and Evelyn Hutchinson; (second row) Carrie Hutchinson Jones, Grace Battey Hutchinson, Lydia Hutchinson, Lovina Hutchinson, Lovina Foote, Alfred W. Hutchinson, Annie Hutchinson Foote, Edward Foote, and Lola Hutchinson holding Alfred Hutchinson; (third row) J. Banks Jones, Arthur Hutchinson, Eva Hutchinson, Doris Hutchinson, Robert Foote, and Carroll Hutchinson.

This tintype from the Pomprowicz collection depicts Horace Fuller Porter, his wife, Mary Bissell Porter, and their seven children. Like most tintypes of the post–Civil War era, some figures are in sharp focus, while others are blurred. Horace was born in 1831 and died in 1912. Mary was born in 1838 and died in 1921. Given the ages of the children shown, this tintype was probably taken between 1870 and 1875.

This wonderful tintype from the Ely collection shows Daisy White, daughter of Edward and Helen Hills White. Like many others, she attended Willimantic Normal School and became a teacher. Daisy returned to Hebron in 1920 to take care of her father, and worked as a teacher at the Jones Street School until 1923. She never married and lived on the family farm, off Paper Mill Road, until her death.

John Edmund Horton and Vivian Shirley Lajoie married on September 8, 1945, and are pictured here at their wedding reception. Lajoie was a microbiologist; Horton was a prominent member of the Douglas Library board of directors and spearheaded the 1957 library addition. The Hortons had three sons: Gregory, Gary, and James. Gary Horton carried on the family tradition by serving as chairman of the library directors, overseeing the second enlargement of the building in 2000.

Della E. Wilcox Porter Hills, born in 1875, is shown in this rare photograph from the Pomprowicz collection. Della served as Hebron's town clerk for almost 17 years. At the time of her death, at age 96, she was the oldest member of the First Congregational Church. She served as organist and Sunday school teacher during her 80-year membership at the church. Della is buried in St. Peter's Cemetery.

Albert Wallace Hilding married Ethel Helen Porter on July 31, 1917. Albert's family were Swedish immigrants who ultimately purchased a farm in Columbia, Connecticut. While in Columbia, they attended the First Congregational Church, and became friends with Charles Bissell. After the Hildings sold the Columbia farm and moved back to New York, they found that they missed the rural life. So, in 1914, the Hilding brothers purchased land on Church Street from Bissell.

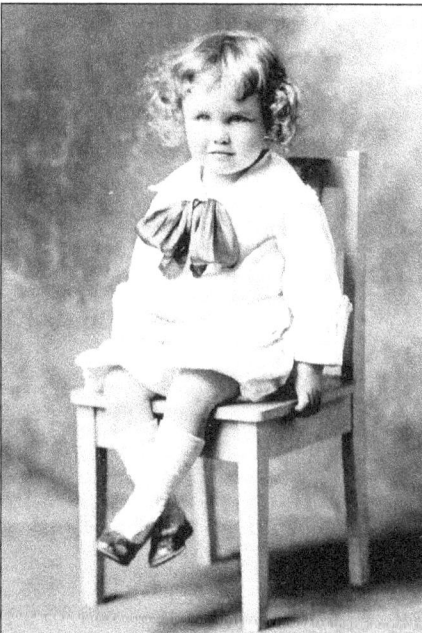

Pictured here in 1920 is Winthrop Edward Hilding, Albert and Ethel Porter Hilding's only son. He went on to be a full professor in mechanical engineering and thermodynamics at the University of Connecticut. Win and his wife, Dolores, now live in Storrs, but he remains actively involved in Hebron history. Not only has he just completed a history of the Fuller-Porter-Hilding family, but he also frequently communicates with his former doctoral candidates.

Alberta Caroline Hilding, shown here in 1922, was the first daughter born to Albert and Ethel Porter Hilding. Alberta earned a degree in accounting and went on to be vice president of investments at Connecticut Bank and Trust. She is active in local community organizations, and still lives in the family's second homestead, off Route 66.

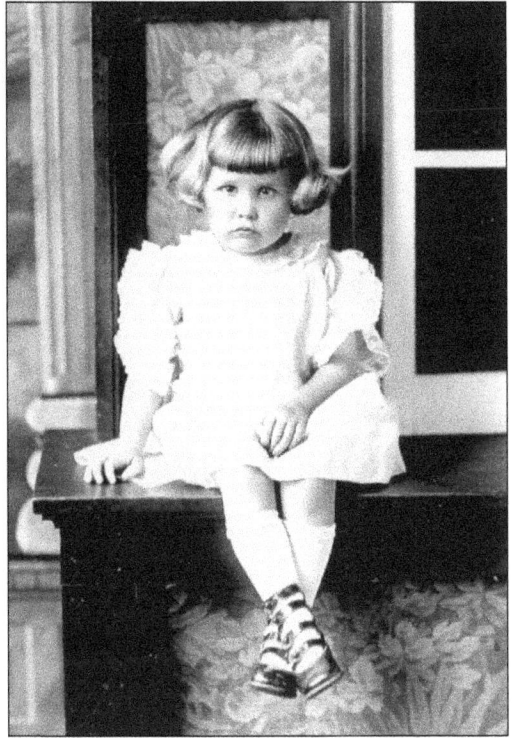

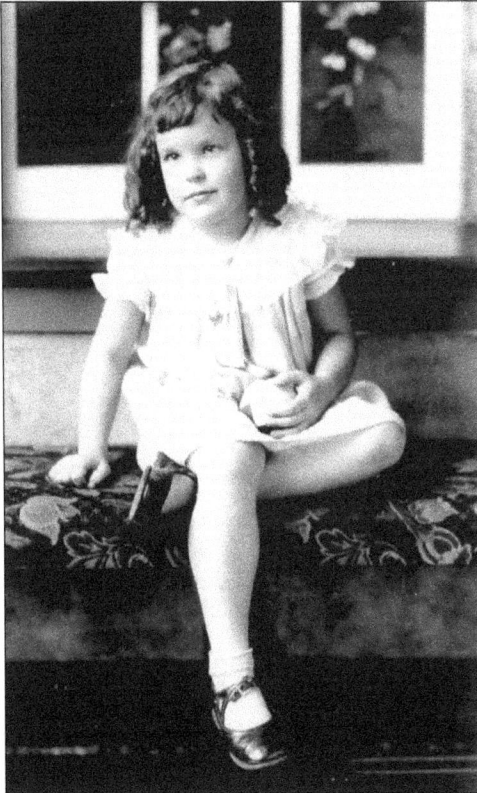

Lois Strong Hilding, the second daughter of Albert and Ethel Porter Hilding, was born in 1926. This photograph from the Hilding collection shows Lois at age four. She received a degree in English from the University of Connecticut, and taught briefly at the Horace Porter School in Columbia, before moving to Pratt's human resources department. In 1956 Lois married Dr. Edward Gerber Jr., a practicing surgeon at Waterbury Hospital.

Winthrop Strong Porter, the second son of Henry Clinton and Annie Strong Porter, married Ethel Louise Hills on August 1, 1917. The Porters (pictured here) had four children: Douglas, Lucille, Wilbur, and Henry. Winthrop was first selectman for many years. During World War II, he was vice president of the Hebron War Council, and also was a long-serving member of the library's board of trustees.

Susan Bingham Pendleton, daughter of Dr. Cyrus Pendleton, was born in 1870 and died on April 3, 1972, just shy of her 102nd birthday. Shown here in 1892, Pendleton was a graduate of the Willimantic Normal School. She was a popular figure by the time of this photograph, being an active member of the Hebron Library Association and a promising writer. Susan wrote for numerous newspapers, including the *Hartford Times* and the *Manchester Herald*.

William Clifford Robinson, pictured here, was born in 1863, and was one of the most progressive farmers in the area. He married Jennie Eliza Leonard during the blizzard of 1888, and they made the trip to the church by sled. Horace Welton Porter walked 10 miles on snowshoes to be the best man at their wedding. Robinson later became a deacon of the Hebron Congregational Church.

The town was pleased when Della Wilcox agreed to marry Roger Porter, shown here c. 1900, courtesy of the Pomprowicz collection. They were a handsome couple and the center of attention at Amston picnics. The Porters lived in the home now occupied by the Maffessoli family, across the road from the Hilding farm (now Church of the Holy Family). Della was considered a leader in preserving Hebron town history.

Dr. Charles Douglas, shown in this c. 1890 photograph, was born in 1860. Douglas, in addition to his association with the Hebron Library, was well known for his sanitarium in Boston, and was also active in other Boston community organizations. Douglas is considered a leader in psychology, as his papers and presentations attest. His love for Ida Porter, whom he ultimately married, is legendary.

Cunningham Photographers of Willimantic, Connecticut, recorded this image of Ida Porter Douglas c. 1880. Ida, a founding member of the Hebron Library Association, eventually married Dr. Charles Douglas. When Douglas bequeathed the bulk of his estate to the library association in 1947, he asked that the building be named in memory of his late wife and her lifetime dedication to Hebron's library.

Wilbur Newton Hills is considered the founder of the Hills Dairy Farms business. He married Annie Post in 1890. The Posts, pictured here, were among the community's first settlers, and they ran a general store and post office in Hebron Center. Hills bought 102 acres from cousin Ellen Brown in 1895. The Browns' land ownership dated back to 1708, when Joshua Sachem, son of Mohegan tribe great sachem Uncas, deeded his lands to the Old Saybrook Legatees. Wilbur and Annie had two children, Homer and Ethel. Ethel married Winthrop Strong Porter, and they began their own farm nearby.

Edward Ashley Smith, shown here in 1918 with his bride, Annie Palmer, was a prolific poet. In honor of the event, Smith wrote "The Time of My Proposal," which states, in part: "We will live by a beautiful river, and the scenery will be grand. We'll have the nicest company that there is in all the land." Ed and Annie had three children: Bradford, Edwin, and Marie.

Edward and Annie Smith are pictured in 1921 with sons Bradford and Edwin. Smith loved Hebron: "To live here in Hebron is a wonderful life. Where everyone likes you, and you love your wife! Where neighbors are neighbors and kindness is there, you'll find for yourself and plenty to spare. So if you don't like us as you move 'round about, pack up your belongings, I advise, and get out!"

Annie Palmer Smith, with her youngest child, Marie Purington, is shown here in an early 1923 photograph from the Billard collection. Edward Smith wrote a poem he entitled "The Truth" about his beloved daughter: "We loved sweet Marie since the time of her birth. And we thank the dear Lord that she came down to earth."

Everett G. Lord is obviously enjoying his ride on the goat cart in this 1932 photograph from the Robinson collection. Grandson Donald Robinson is shown on the right, patiently but eagerly awaiting his turn. The Lord's Red Barn is shown in the background; the First Congregational Church now owns the barn.

Pictured here in 1920, John Horton is shown with his aunt Elizabeth Doyle as they play in the south yard of Governor Peter's house. Notice the fence in the background, which was at least 100 years old at the time the photograph was taken. Because the main users of Church Street were cattle and other livestock, the fence was important for directing traffic.

Annie Hutchinson, shown here in 1905, is wearing the dress that was made for her graduation reception from Bacon Academy in Colchester. In addition to being proficient in Latin, German, and French, Annie wrote the lyrics to *Baconia* (Bacon Academy's alma mater), which is still used today. The chorus proclaims: "Baconia, we love thee! To thee we will sing, in summer and autumn, in winter and spring."

Dr. Charles Douglas is shown here in 1907. According to the Sibun book, Douglas's "mother had been a White, who was directly descended from the famous Peregrine of that name—'first white baby born in the new world.' The Whites had arrived on the Mayflower." Despite his successful medical practice in Boston, he was very active in establishing the Hebron Library Association (precursor to the board of trustees).

Lucius Waterman Robinson married Mary Adelaide Lord in 1918. They are pictured here in 1925 with their two sons Lucius Jr. (age 3) and Donald (age 6 months). The Lords were active in Hebron community affairs; their original homestead consisted of the lands north of today's Route 66. Robinson's family had moved from Lebanon to Hebron in 1839; Lucius was a part-time farmer and full-time banker for the Federal Land Bank.

Shown here at age 49, Susan B. Pendleton is famous for her book of poetry, *They Will Remain*, published in 1966 on her 95th birthday. She wrote: "At this I marvel. I shall be gone . . . I must believe it. There will be, still, Burrows Hill tarrying, Gilead Hill, Dug Hill, and Burnt Hill, and Meeting House Lane . . . Quiet, unchanging, they will remain." Pendleton never married. She is buried at St. Peter's.

Susan Pendleton's fame has centered on her reputation as a teacher and poet, yet she was also an accomplished artist. Using pencil and charcoal, she sketched no fewer than 15 portraits of her family members. At 32, she created a haunting self-portrait, seen here for the first time, courtesy of the Robinson collection. Pendleton once wrote: "I was always afraid of the world. But I looked it in the eye."

In this 1936 photograph, Elizabeth Mary Horton enjoys a ride on her horse at her grandmother's house (next to the Hebron Records Building). Horton was a nun with the Sisters of Mercy for over 25 years and taught at various schools, including Mercy High School in Middletown and St. Joseph's College, where she was ultimately named dean of women. Her father, Edmund H. Horton, and brother, John E. Horton, both served as Hebron selectmen.

The editors of Annie Hutchinson's 1912 Alfred University senior yearbook wrote: "Annie, Annie! Oh that name is written in our halls of fame. Oh, 'twould be a crying shame if our Anne should change her name." But she did exactly that when she married Robert Foote in 1913. The couple, pictured here, lived in Suffield and Chester, where Rob was the high school principal, before they returned to Foothills Farm in 1919 to resume farming.

Young Henry Jones is shown in this 1922 photograph with his father, Frank, and his great-grandmother Melissa Hills Jones. Melissa was born on October 21, 1840, and married Flavel Jones in 1856. The Joneses had eight children, and lived in the Bradford house, which bordered the Hebron and Marlborough town lines. The house burned down in the early 1960s. Henry, like other young Hebron men of his era, served in World War II.

Robert Henry Horton, brother to John and Elizabeth, married Doris Rigby. Both were lifelong teachers in Lebanon, and they had seven children. Robert is pictured here riding his horse at his grandmother Horton's house, located next to the Hebron Records Building. A University of Connecticut graduate, Robert also served in the military after World War II.

To longtime residents, he is known as "Carly B." Carlton Blish Jones, pictured here, was the father of Carlton Hills Jones, better known as "Gil," who operated the only garage in Hebron. Carly B. was an auctioneer and Hebron probate judge for many years. Henry Jones remembers that Carly B., in order to stimulate bidding at his auctions, would wave something unusual, such as a chamber pot, and urge people to bid.

Deems Buell was the son of Elton Buell, who had a wood-turning shop on North Street (now owned by a private resident). Deems, who was paid $4.50 a year for being town auditor, followed in his father's footsteps in the wood-turning business, and ultimately relocated it to Laconia, New Hampshire. Deems married Helen Foote, daughter of Edward and Alice (Hills) Foote. This is a photograph from their wedding, which was held in the front parlor at Footehills Farm.

Helen Mae White, pictured left, daughter of Edward and Helen Hills White, went to business school in Hartford, but ended her career and became a farmer's wife when she married Arthur Michael Keefe, pictured below. The Keefes' dairy operation on West Street (near the Glastonbury town line) included 65 cows and was considered a large enterprise. The couple had four children: Helen Margaret, Sherwood Arthur, Stanley Hills, and Marian Louise. Margaret is an active member of the community and the historical society.

Asa Ellis is seen in 1938 with his mother, Emily Webster Ellis, and his sister, Clara M. Ellis, in this photograph, courtesy of the Ellis collection. Asa was a farmer, a state legislator, and a deacon of the Gilead Congregational Church. Clara never married and instead devoted her life to taking care of the ailing and elderly population. She lived in the homestead (now Mapleleaf Farm) all her life.

Pictured here in 1925, the Porter brothers went on to serve in different military branches during World War II. Gordon Earl, in front, became a member of the Marine Corps and earned two bronze stars and a Purple Heart. In the back row are David Kenneth, far left, who served in the U.S. Navy aboard the USS Saratoga; Howard Edgar, center, who served with the U.S. Army 8th Air Force in England; and Leonard Carey, who earned a Distinguished Flying Cross from the U.S. Army Air Corps.

Clarence and Marion White Rathbun, with their daughter Janet, are shown here in 1946. The Rathbuns had a dairy farm on East Street, which continued operations through the 1960s. In addition to Janet, the Rathbuns had two sons, Robert and William. The Rathbuns were extremely active in local groups, including the 4-H Club, the Grange, and other farm organizations.

Dr. Cyrus H. Pendleton moved to Hebron in the 1860s, and practiced medicine there for almost three generations. Pendleton was famous as a scholar and founder of the Hebron Library Association, serving as president from its 1888 inception until 1919. This never-before-published photograph of Pendleton, taken in his home, comes from the Toomey collection. The Toomeys purchased the Pendleton house—also known as "Pendletonia"—in 1980, and now refer to it as "Tara Mara."

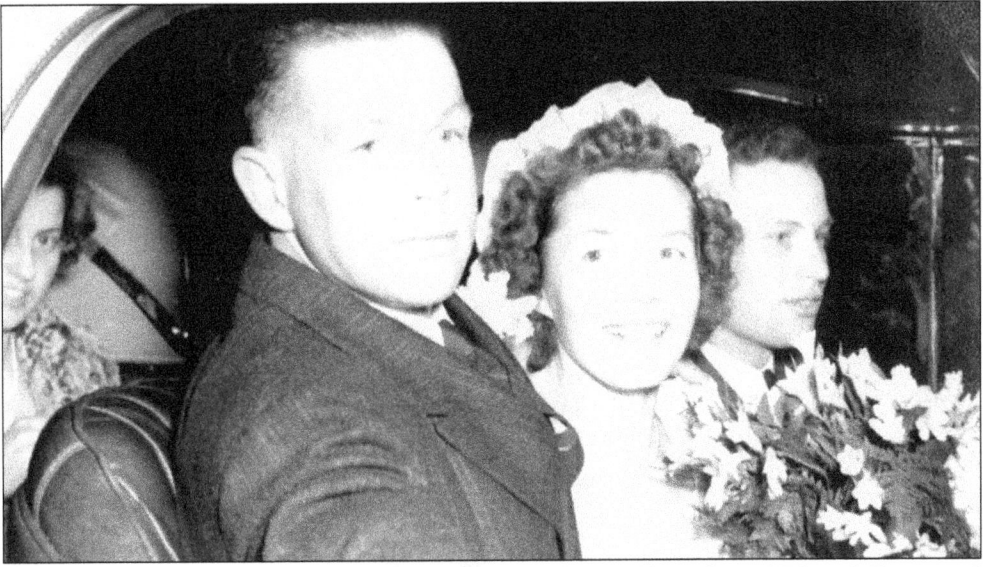

This photograph was taken on March 27, 1943, the wedding day of Edward Foote and Marion Walker Odell. The newlyweds proceeded from the church in this shiny 1941 Pontiac convertible, the last one made before all manufacturing went into the war effort. Ed's brother Robert Hutchinson Foote, shown in the background at right, was best man. Marion's sister Janet Odell Milne is in the back seat; she was matron of honor. The Footes were married for 59 years.

In 1910, Lawrence Pomprowicz, a Polish immigrant, married Anastasia Huk in Newark, New Jersey. The two are shown on their wedding day. Working in a leather factory proved to be bad for Lawrence's health, and he was advised by a doctor to move to a rural community. He and his cousin, John Kowalski, then purchased 320 acres on Wellswood Road, and moved their families to Hebron. Unfortunately, they lost the land during the Depression.

Robert Fuller Porter and Viola Irene Preston were married on July 6, 1919. The Porters had four children: Gibson Clinton (born 1920), Milton Robert (born 1924), Roberta Viola (born 1937), and Virginia Millicent (born 1939). Robert was the first son of Henry Clinton Porter and Annie Strong Porter.

Gerald Fitch Porter and Horace Northam Porter are shown here in this 1926 photograph, courtesy of the Gray collection. They were the first two sons born to Horace Clinton and Helen Mary Jones Porter. In later years, both sons worked for and retired from Pratt & Whitney. Gerry is especially remembered for the horse auctions he held in his barn on East Main Street. The auctions were eagerly anticipated community events.

Merle Natalie Jones and Gordon Earl Porter married in 1946, after Earl returned from the war. Merle graduated from Arnold College in New Haven, where she earned a degree in physical education. A natural athlete, she taught for 30 years and coached basketball and softball at East Hampton High School. Earl graduated from the University of Connecticut with an engineering degree. He was instrumental in the design and building of many famous institutions.

This photograph, from the Pomprowicz collection, was taken on September 19, 1910. Sitting up front are Chester Tennant (at the steering wheel), Harry Tennant, and Harry's son Allyn. In the back seat are Annie Tennant Rathbone (on the left), Harry's daughter Doris, and ? Tennant, the wife of Harry. The Tennants were eager to own an automobile, as family members commuted frequently between East Hampton and the family homestead on Millstream Road in Hebron. The model seen here is a 1908 Stanley Steamer, produced just a few years after the first cars reached the U.S. market in 1903.

The children of Lawrence and Anastasia Pomprowicz are pictured here. From left to right are the following: (first row) Josie, their beloved dog Spot, and Henry; (second row) Jane, Edward, and Sophie. Daughter Sandra was born shortly after the photograph was taken. The children are standing in front of the Pomprowicz home, directly across the road from the Company One fire station. Ultimately, the house was torn down and a strip mall took its place.

Kenneth Waldo Ellis and Dorothy Davidson White, seen here, were married in 1939. Ken was a chicken and dairy farmer. He also ran an insurance business and served on the board of finance for many years. All six of Ken and Dorothy's children are still living: Katherine Ellis Jobin, Edward Armstrong (Ned) Ellis (who still runs Mapleleaf Farm), Gwendolyn Ellis Mund, Christine Webster Ellis Irish, Constance Waldo Ellis Wilson, and Marilyn Louise Ellis Swensen.

This photograph was taken in 1942, Marie Purington Smith's sophomore year at the University of Connecticut. She proudly wears a special guy's coat. At the bottom of the photograph, Marie handwrote a note to her future husband, Albert Barnes Billard: "To the swellest fellow in the world! Lots of love, Marie." Marie and Al married in 1943. She celebrated her 60th class reunion at UConn in 2004.

Norman Jewett Warner's children are shown here in this mid-1920s photograph from the Raymond collection. They are, from left to right, Norton Perry, William Hutchinson, Olive, Allene Keables, and Charlotte Isabel. Sister Jean Lydia was too young for the photograph, and brother Alden Talcott had not yet been born. Their grandfather, William Jewett Warner, was the state's dairy food commissioner, and the photograph was used to promote drinking milk for children's health.

In 1905, Annie Hutchinson was accepted with a full scholarship to Mount Holyoke College in Massachusetts. Due to the ill health of her sister-in-law, Annie stayed home to care for her, and worked as a teacher at a Hebron school. In 1908 Annie enrolled in Alfred University in New York, and in 1912 she became the first Hebron woman to graduate from a four-year university. In 1970, she wrote a book of history called *In Gilead*.

Two

THE FARMS

This 1920s view of the Footehills Farm depicts the Foote boys mowing hay. Footehills Farm still cuts hay three times a year, from May to September. In this image, the field where the hay is being gathered shows stone walls; those have since been cleared to create a 20-acre field. The field borders the Marlborough and Glastonbury town lines. This scene calls to mind Dorothy Taggart's poem "Haying Time": "The easy flowing meter of his swing as the high grass fell; Air, fragrant with essence of hay; A sweet tremolo to the familiar tune he whistled in concert with lazy crickets and locust in the grass."

This aerial view of the Hilding farm shows the homestead and all the barns. Clarence Bissell, who had befriended Hilding brothers Charles, Samuel, Edward, and Albert, sold this land to them in 1914. The Hildings spent the first year clearing a portion of the land and building the shed. Today, the Church of the Holy Family owns much of the property, including the house, which has been turned into a parsonage.

Claude Jones displays his prized pulling oxen, Chub and Dan, in this 1929 photograph. Shortly before the 1938 hurricane, he sold his Wall Street dairy and purchased the Rathbun dairy farm on Marjorie Circle. A prominent democrat, Jones served as Hebron's first selectman for a total of eight years. His wife, Natalie Blume Jones, a prominent democrat who served in the Connecticut legislature, was also the longtime organist at St. Peter's.

Butchering time, though distasteful to many, was a fact of life on Hebron farms. In this 1910 photograph from the Raymond collection, George Hills and John Gilbert attend to the slaughter of hogs. The large half-barrels would hold the entrails, which would be recycled in a variety of ways. George Hills was Wilbur Porter's great-grandfather.

This amazing view of the Porter Farm is from the Porter collection. Located to the east of these farm buildings (just out of view at the bottom), is the family homestead—a structure that for decades was the largest blacksmith shop in the area. The house has been carefully restored and preserves much of Hebron's history. Horses and oxen were routinely shod at the shop; the Porters have the original ledgers from the mid-1800s that show the daily entries for all transactions.

In a dairy community, refrigeration was a concern. This contraption is an old-time ice-cutting machine. Families went out to ponds in the winter, marked straight lines on the frozen surface, and used the machine to cut blocks of ice. The blocks were then loaded on a wagon and taken to an icehouse. Inside, the blocks were carefully laid and packed tightly with sawdust to fill in any air holes. If stored correctly, unused ice would have barely melted by the end of summer.

No farm in the late 1800s and early 1900s could exist without a saw rig. The machine took a variety of shapes and forms, depending on the engineering skills of the family members. This 1937 photograph depicts the Foote saw rig. Land was cleared manually, and the saw rig would then cut the downed trees into useful firewood.

Today, tall trees obscure the view of the original Smith Farm on Burrows Hill Road. This 1940 photograph from the Billard collection gives an expansive view of the homestead. On the right is the easily recognizable home of Edward and Annie Smith, resplendent with its Grecian columns. In the foreground is Florence Smith, with her apple pick for the day, lovingly touching the head of her faithful dog, Bob.

Clarence E. Porter plows a garden spot on the Pendleton land with Claude Jones's oxen team, Tom and Jerry. The Hebron Center School (now the American Legion) stands in the background. As this 1944 photograph so eloquently illustrates, Clarence was deep in thought. All four of his sons were far from home, serving in various branches of the U.S. military, leaving him to do his work in solitude.

In 1947, Ed and Marion Foote look over a cornfield on their dairy farm. They hold their two oldest children, Mary Ann and John. The young couple were busy raising a family and operating a large, progressive dairy farm. Both Ed and Marion were involved in a variety of state, town, and community affairs.

Mapleleaf Farm has been in the Ellis family for generations. Edward (Ned) and Renee Ellis still live in the original homestead and run their progressive dairy operation. The family's poultry operations ended in the early 1960s; this photograph shows the old coops. Residents can always identify Mapleleaf Farm in October, when the family conducts self-service pumpkin sales.

No child, male or female, was excused from daily chores. This never-before-seen photograph shows Marie Smith tending the cows on the family farm in 1938. The old barn in the background burned down in 1974.

Many Hebron residents feed the local deer, especially as housing developments continue to displace these gentle creatures. This is not a new practice, as this photograph can attest; here, Robert Hutchinson Foote is shown feeding Deerie. The Foote family photograph albums are filled with pictures of both Bob and Ed Foote with Deerie, whom they fed from infancy to adulthood. Even today, the family keeps a watchful eye on every aspect of wildlife on their farm.

The Hills family provided this wonderful aerial view of their farm; Gilead Street (Route 85) divides the farmland on the right. Wilbur Hills and his wife, Annie Post Hills, bought the property from his cousin Ellen Brown in 1895. Alan and Denise Hills still operate the dairy today. While the total farm consists of 230 acres, only 90 acres are tillable. The family still lives in the original farmhouse that was built in 1740.

This 1908 photograph from the Raymond collection depicts the barn-raising event for the Warner barn, which still stands on Gilead Street. Notice the formal dress of those participating in the event—three-piece suits, neckwear, and even hats are worn by most of the workers. The clothing speaks volumes as to the formality of such community events, even when hard labor was involved.

48

In 1942, the Smith family witnessed the birth of twin calves, shown here with Edward Smith in an original photograph from the Billard collection. While it was an exciting moment for the Smith children, such an event is not usually looked upon with favor by dairy farmers. According to *Dairy Biz*, "Cows carrying twins face increased health risks . . . they take longer to breed back once the calves are born."

The Hills homestead was built *c.* 1740 by Dr. William Sumner; the original front porch, torn down in 1970, is shown here. Sumner was granted three parcels of Joshua Sachem's land from the Old Saybrook Legatees. In the 1800s the land was owned by the Browns, then was sold to Wilbur Newton Hills in 1895. Wilbur was a hometown boy, who lived on what is now Martin Road most of his life.

In this photograph, we see a silo that was used to hold green grass. The grass would ferment while in storage, and then be used to feed the animals in the winter. This is a different procedure than what is commonly associated with hay. Also shown is a 1935 International truck loaded with dry hay, which would be moved to the barn, unbaled. The tractor is a 15W30, an early model that came equipped with steel wheels.

C. Daniel Way was 79 years old when this photograph, from the Ellis collection, was taken in 1947. He was still an active cattle dealer even then. A hired hand managed Way's farmlands while he managed the cattle side of the operations. He and his wife, Lida, owned the farm next to Mapleleaf, the Ellis farm. Way was famous for always driving big Cadillacs and attending almost all community functions.

This never-before-published photograph from the Billard collection was taken in the late 1930s. It features Florence Smith, who by now was in her 40s and a highly respected educator, still out doing farm chores. Mabel Payson and her friend are shown in the background, horsing around with an old tire. The Smith Farm was a combined dairy, orchard, and poultry operation until 1960.

In this scene from 1948, Ed Foote drives the old 15W30 tractor while pulling a handmade stoneboat through the farmyard. Stoneboats were used to clear land and for other heavy tasks. Two of Foote's children, Mary Ann and John, show sheer delight with their ride aboard the stoneboat. Farm families worked hard together in this agrarian community, and often a change of pace—such as this ride—made everyone's day a lot more fun.

In 1927, Elizabeth Doyle snapped this photograph of her nephew John Horton, with one of his favorite cows. Like all children of the time, chores were a part of life for this youngster. Horton became active in local politics, serving as a selectman during the 250th anniversary of Hebron, a charter member of the zoning commission, and an original member of the Douglas Library board of trustees when that board was established in 1950.

Pictured here is the third barn to grace the Hills Farm; it was built in 1930, after the first two barns burned down. This barn suffered damage in the great hurricane of 1938, but the structure was repairable and still stands today. The Hills Farm is a 230-acre dairy operation; Alan and Denise Hills, carrying on the family tradition, have 170 cows that produce 6,000 pounds of milk a day.

Robert E. Foote is shown leading a team of horses in the 1930s. It may be Queenie and Dan, a team that served the farm family for many years. Robert's attire is not fancy, undoubtedly patched and very comfortable—and quite different from the way he dressed when appearing as a state legislator, commissioner of domestic animals, and chairman of both the Republican town committee and the board of education.

A young Kenneth Ellis handles a large team of horses as he rakes hay. Occasionally, a horse would get stung or spooked and would bolt, upsetting the equipment and injuring the rider in the process. Chores were integral to the smooth operation of the family farm. It was expected that one son would stay on the farm and pass it on to future generations. Kenneth, a good son, did just that.

This photograph shows the backside of the old Fuller-Porter gristmill. The mill's water wheel was sold to Old Sturbridge Village in 1938, and it is now part of the historical display. Sturbridge Village also obtained the millstones and flour stones from the site. According to Winthrop Hilding, the flour stones had been imported from France.

Clarence White, the son of Edward and Helen Hills White, is shown here in 1931 with his two favorite cows. He also worked in the family's wood business. Clarence, like his sister Daisy, never married, and he lived with his parents all his life at the White family farm on Paper Mill Road in Amston.

Three

THE BUSINESSES

This photograph depicts the Hewitt store c. 1908. Celebrations for the town's bicentennial abounded at the time of this picture. Notice the reference to "Pump Town"—the name dates back to the period following the French and Indian War, when the townspeople created a cannon from a tree log (a "pump") to celebrate the victory. The pump blew up the first time it was fired; since then Hebron has been nicknamed Pump Town. A water pump is mistakenly featured in the official town logo.

The bustling train depot in Turnerville (now Amston), is shown here in early 1900. Travelers made connections here between New York and Boston, and the station boosted the local economy. The Amston Inn was always filled, and Ira Turschen's store did good business. Henry Jones relates an interesting story about the Turnerville line: Whenever the train needed to go to Colchester, it made the trip in reverse—there was no turnaround at the Turnerville depot.

This rare photograph from the Pomprowicz collection depicts the Amston Inn, which was located just north of the old Turnerville Railroad Depot. The inn was always busy, especially as the depot became a major stopover for those headed east to Boston or west to New York. Visitors sat on the front porch, watching passing traffic. One of the stone posts seen in the foreground still stands today.

Carlton Hills "Gil" Jones ran a popular, and the only, garage in town in the 1930s and 1940s. The garage was located in the vicinity of today's florist shop, just east of the old town hall. Pictured here is the original 1937 Hebron fire truck, parked out front of Gil's garage. Apparently, the fire truck also needed a little tune-up.

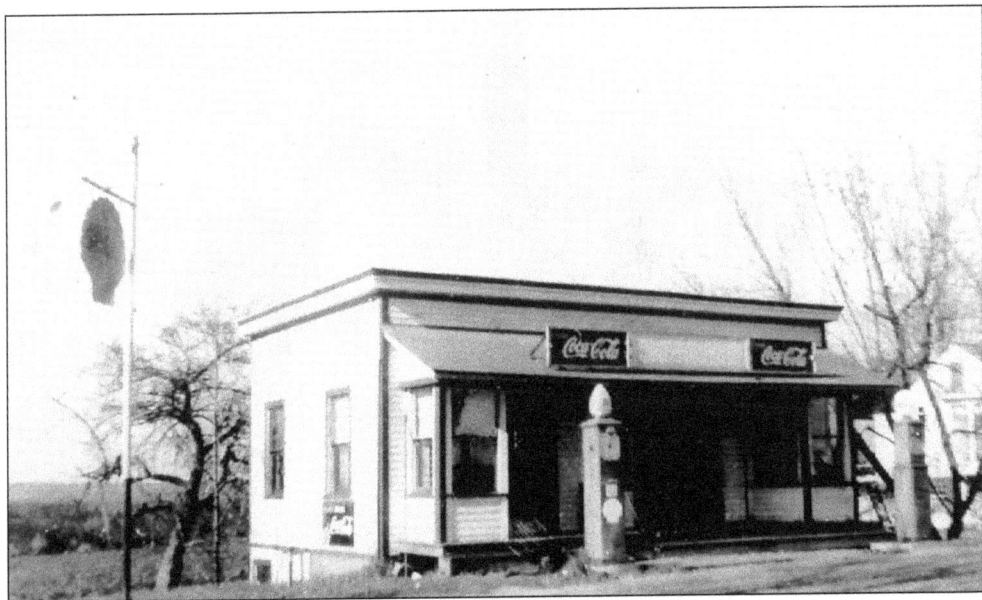

This photograph from the Raymond collection was taken in 1939. It's a view of the Clarence J. Fogil store, formerly located in the area of what is now Gilead Street and Porter Road, which operated from the 1930s through the 1950s. Clarence's son, Floyd A. Fogil Sr., also ran the store during this period. The store sold Texaco gasoline and small items such as milk and bread.

Located on South Church Street in Amston, this was Ira Turshen's store and grain mill. The mill is seen on the right-hand side of the building; the general store is on the left. The proximity to the Turnerville railroad station, about a quarter of a mile away, was quite convenient for Turshen's operations.

The Hills's private collection includes this photograph of the Hubbell Creamery. From Annie Foote's *In Gilead* we learn: "A milk receiving station was built on Wilbur Hills's land by M. B. and F. S. Hubbell of New Haven. Here, the milk, which had been cooled at the farm, was brought to a lower temperature, transported by a two-horse team to Turnerville (now Amston), and shipped by train to New Haven."

The Great Northern Survey Company of Albany, New York, came through town in 1894 and took a photograph of the H. E. Emmons store, located on the southeast corner of the Green. Notice the sign on the left advertising "Choice Pickled Red Salmon" for sale. Subsequently the business became the Hewitt store; today the building is known as the Hewitt House, and it serves as the offices of McCorrison D. W. Fish.

This photograph was taken in 1918 and is provided courtesy of the Pomprowicz collection. The Tennants were well-known, popular residents. This is a view inside one of several stores the family ran in the Green area. Harry Tennant ran a photograph shop in Hebron, and another in East Hampton. Here, the children are tending the store.

This photograph, from the Pomprowicz collection, was taken on July 24, 1888. By then, the Charles Post store had been sold to L. H. Leon. The post office continued to operate from the store. Like the Emmons store, Leon sold pickled salmon. Eggs were 22 cents a dozen, which seems high for a community with so many poultry farms. Notice the woman looking out the second-floor center window.

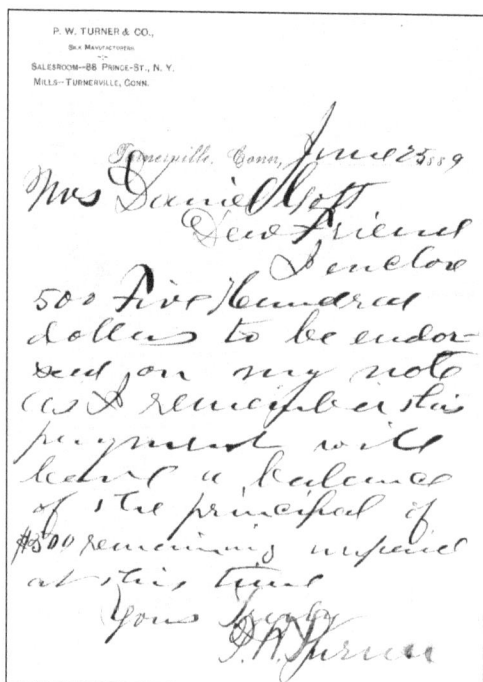

P. W. Turner had some debts, as evidenced by this original 1889 letter from the Horton collection. He wrote to Sally Bailey Gott (Mrs. Daniel Gott): "Dear Friend: I enclose 500 Five Hundred dollars to be endorse'ed on my note as I remember this payment will leave a balance of the principal of $500 remaining unpaid at this time. Yours truly, P. W. Turner." Turner later sold his mills and land to Charles Ams.

Henry Jones remembers an exciting time when the federal government raided the distillery in Amston in the 1930s. According to the legend, liquor was taxed based on labels, not the number of bottles manufactured or sold. So the distillery's operators hid the labels under the floorboards to avoid paying taxes. Pictured are some confiscated labels, courtesy of the Amston Liquor Shoppe. After the raid, a businessman took over the distillery and ran it in accordance with the tax laws.

The longtime head weaver and manager of P. W. Turner's silk mill in Amston was Edward White, who is shown here in 1918 with wife Ellen Hills White and granddaughter Helen Margaret Keefe. In the background is the White homestead on Paper Mill Road in Amston. The woodpile contains large logs that eventually will be cut by the White men and then sold in their wood business.

This original 1807 photograph has been recaptured on numerous postcards. In this westward view toward Marlborough, the elm tree in Hebron Center is shown, as are the home and store that eventually became associated with the Charles Post family. However, the name Rathbun is clearly shown on the storefront. Major Post purchased the buildings in 1832, at which time he renamed the store. The Kellogg house is shown on the far right.

This original stock certificate, for 10 shares in the Sterling Automobile Manufacturing Company, comes from the Henry Jones collection. By October 1916, all 100,000 shares of stock in the company had been sold, mostly to New Yorkers. Charles Ams only owned 3,102 shares; a Rose Einbund purchased 46,199 shares. No Hebron or Amston resident invested in the company, despite local hopes and expectations for success.

Four

THE CHURCHES

This photograph of the north side of St. Peter's Church was taken *c.* 1880. According to the *History of St. Peter's Episcopal Church*: "Sometime in the 19th century the exterior brick was painted white; at that time whitewashing brick exteriors was thought appropriate to buildings which seemed vaguely Colonial . . . the white paint on St. Peter's, simply by not being periodically renewed, has slowly disintegrated, leaving the original color red and texture."

This original photograph from the Robinson collection was taken in 1883. The great fire of April 17, 1882, burned down much of Hebron Center, including the Congregational church. According to church history, Ida Porter wrote: "Only the pulpit, the pulpit chairs, the Bible and the hymn book, and three choir chairs were saved. All the rest with our nice organ has gone to ashes."

Transportation to church became a problem in the early 1800s. The north side of town was growing rapidly, but residents had to travel many miles to attend church in the center of Hebron. In bad weather and with poor road conditions, it could take hours to get to church by horse and buggy. The Gilead Church was finally built and dedicated in 1838. It shared the same minister with the Hebron Congregational Church, thereby making the two congregations yoked.

In another delightful tintype from the Pomprowicz collection, the Austin family buggy is shown here, c. 1880. The Gilead Congregational Church is visible in the background at the far left. Notice that Gilead Street (now Route 85) is still the old dirt road, and that fences line all the properties. Since Gilead Street was a frequent passageway for livestock, the fences kept errant herds in line.

The Austin family buggy didn't visit the Gilead Congregational Church only. It also visited the First Congregational Church's rededication in 1883, after the church was rebuilt following the great fire. A careful examination of the two tintypes on this page reveals that it is the same horse and buggy in both images.

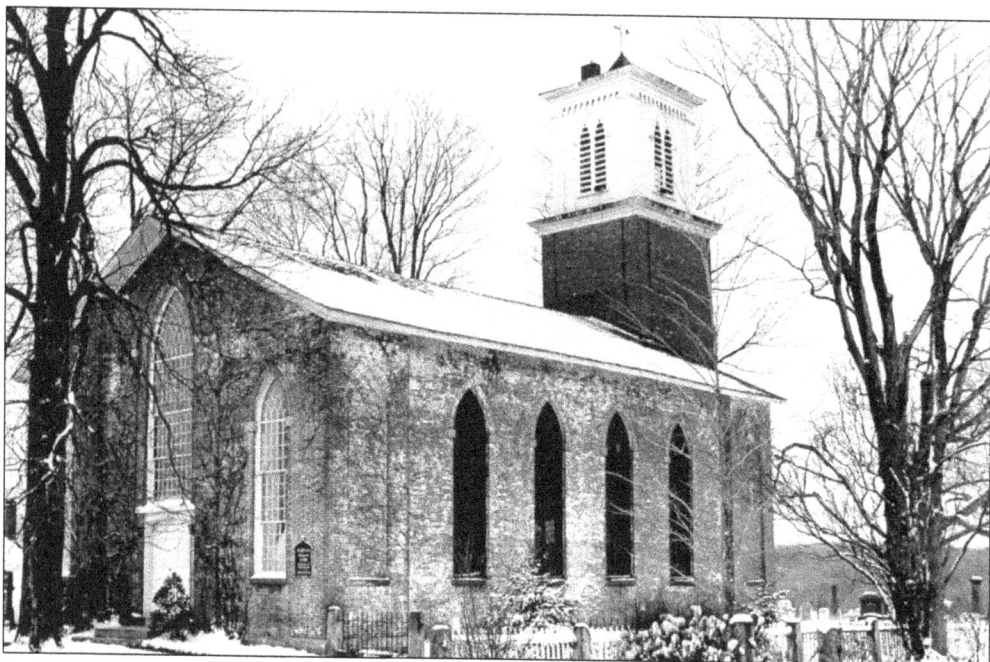

St. Peter's Episcopal Church was built and consecrated in 1826. The clay for the bricks probably came from Millstream Road, as it is the same type of brick as that used for the Peters and Waldo (now Pomprowicz) homes. By 1915, the white paint from the 1800s was starting to fade naturally on the red bricks. Only occasionally can one find flecks of white paint there today.

This photograph, dated 1915 by Mrs. J. H. Williams, depicts the First Congregational Church. An unknown resident is shown with his horse-drawn buggy in front of the church. According to church records, "In 1915 the first annual roll call and dinner occurred" after the church was incorporated. "From time to time improvements were made such as painting, installation of an organ blower, a new roof, lavatories, and other facilities."

Considered an exemplary work of art deco, especially for northeastern Connecticut, the United Brethren of Hebron Synagogue on Church Street was built in 1940, just south of the old town green. The building project was particularly successful thanks to the tireless efforts of Ira Turshen, owner of a general store and grain mill in Amston. The synagogue features a Mediterranean-Gothic doorway with Tudor/Moorish arched side lights.

To all people to whom these presents shall come,--- *Greeting*

WHEREAS, the Society of the *Protestant Episcopal Church* in Hebron, in the County of Tolland, commonly called St. Peter's Church, on the 28th day of March A. D. 1828, passed a vote in the words following, viz:

Voted—That the Treasurer of this Society be and he is hereby authorized to sell and make proper conveyances of the lots in the Burying Ground, contiguous to this Church, and that the avails of said lots shall be, and are appropriated to the purchase of a Church Bell.

NOW KNOW YE, THAT I, *Frederic P. Bissell*

as Treasurer of said Society by virtue and in pursuance of said vote, in consideration of *Seven* dollars received of *Chauncey Gott* for the use of said Society, do hereby sell and convey unto *the said Gott* the following lot or parcel of said Burying Ground, viz:

Lot No 85

To have and hold said lot unto him the said *Gott* and to his heirs and assigns forever, to be used only for burying the dead.

In testimony whereof, for, and in behalf of said Society, I have set my hand and seal this *2"* day of *July* A. D. *1864*

Signed, Sealed, and Delivered, in presence of *Almira L. Bissell* *Frederic P. Bissell* ---- Treasurer
F. Eleanor Bissell of the Protestant Episcopal Society in Hebron.

TOLLAND COUNTY ss. HEBRON, *July 2" 1864*

Personally appeared *Frederic P. Bissell* Treasurer of the Protestant Society in Hebron, and acknowledged the foregoing instrument to be his free act and deed, — before me *Jonathan G. Page Judge Probate*

Chauncy Gott was born in 1802, and the Horton family counts him among their ancestors. On July 2, 1864, Frederick P. Bissell submitted this official document to Jonathan Page, the probate judge, affirming that Gott had purchased a plot at the St. Peter's Cemetery for the sum of seven dollars. The probate judge was required to sign off on the sale of any cemetery plots. This never-before-seen document is courtesy of the Horton collection.

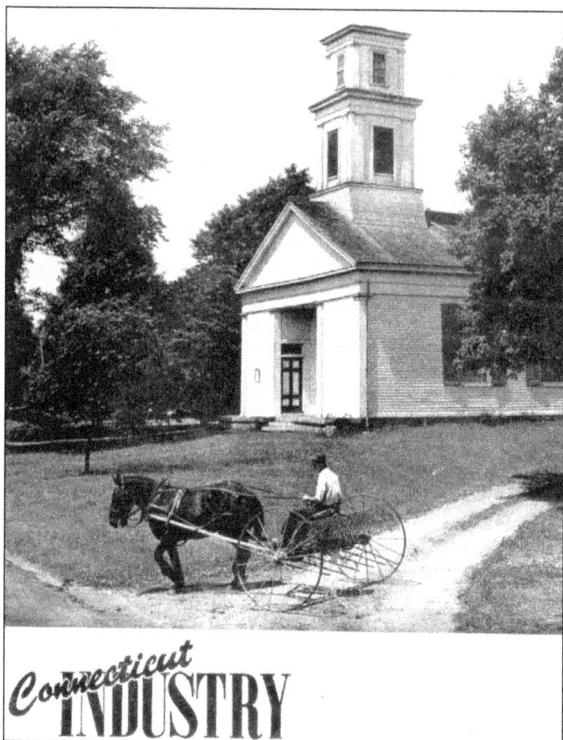

This photograph of the Gilead Congregational Church, taken in 1947, graced the cover of *Connecticut Industry* magazine in August 1948. The editor wrote: "Reminiscent of the slower tempo of pre-automobile days, this month's front cover scene of the old colonial church was snapped by photographer Josef Scaylea as he was passing the village of Gilead, Connecticut last summer."

This original copy of the song Susan Pendleton wrote in 1926 was in tune with the times. According to the *History of St. Peter's Episcopal Church*, "Much attention was given always to the church music, for the rector during most of this time 1919–1929, the Rev. Theodore D. Martin, was a well-known composer of hymns who had sung in some of the first American performances of Gilbert and Sullivan's operettas."

Written for
the 100th Anniversary of
The Present St. Peter's Church Building.

Words by
SUSAN B. PENDLETON, 1926

St. Peter's, Hebron
T. D. MARTIN, 1926

This earth-ly house our fath-ers built,

This tem-ple reared to Thee. Oh, Je-sus, shed on

it the light Of Thy be-nig-ni-ty. A-men.

2.
Bless Thou its altar, roof and tower,
Bless Thou its open door,
Bless Thou the souls that enter here,
And keep them evermore.

3.
There needeth not a house of stone
That souls may lift in prayer;
One humble heart that pleads alone,
Jesus, Thou wilt be there.

4.
There needeth not a temple built,
Which earthly hands did rear,
The heart must bow, the heart must melt,
And, Jesus, Thou wilt hear.

5.
Yet faithful ones still cry to Thee,
Bless Thou this ancient shrine,
Bless Thou its venerable walls,
And hold it ever Thine.

Five

THE SCHOOLS

This photograph of Hebron Center School students is from the Jones-Porter collection. From left to right are the following: (first row) Leonard Rockmillawitz, Raphael Kassman, Tony Gonci, John Kulynyck, Tyke Kowalski, Carlton Jones, Earl Porter, Abe Sherman, and unidentified; (second row) Jane Pomprowicz, Barbara Tennant, Lillian Griffing, Irving Griffin, Joseph Kowalski, unidentified, and Bradford Smith; (third row) Betty Gonci, Marcia Frankel, Laura Jones, Kate Kulynyck, Gertrude Jones, Elsie Hills, John Kowalski, Edwin Smith, Helen Ives, Elsie Garbich, Alberta Hilding, Henry Pomprowicz, and Gibson Porter; (fourth row) Aceynath Jones, Dorothy Gray, Jean Ives, unidentified, Gordon Rathbun, George Gonci, Frank Kulynyck, and Bill Griffin.

According to the October 31, 1894 entry in Ella Smith's diary, this photograph depicts teacher Eloise Ellis of Gilead, shown far left, at the Burrows Hill School. The children are, from left to right, Bessie Peters, Walter Wright, Emily Hanna, Henry Andre, Edna Smith, and Edward A. Smith. The Hebron Historical Society now owns this one-room schoolhouse, which is believed to be the oldest in Hebron and was maintained for years by Edward A. Smith.

Students and staff at Gilead Hill School are pictured here in 1894. From left to right are the following: (first row) Frank Banning, Annie Hutchinson, Fred Banning, Frank Prentice, and Eddie Swan; (second row) Jessie Post, Miss ? Twining (teacher), Arthur Prentice, Clifford Perry, Harold Post, Norman Warner, Alfred Way, Myron Gilbert, Miss ? Williams (visiting teacher), and Clara Root; (third row) ? Hutchinson (son of George), Florence Way, Carroll Hutchinson, and Florence Banning; (fourth row) Cassius Way, Edna Post, and Clarence Prentice.

This original graduation booklet from the Billard collection is dated December 25, and it was printed for the Hebron High School class of 1905. It features teacher James Herbert Clark on the cover. The names of students listed within are all recognizable family names: Buell, Foote, Frink, Goldberg, Hanna, Holbrook, Hewitt, Horton, Lord, Lubchansky, Perry, Porter, Post, Robinson, Shekhetobb, Smith, Spencer, and Wright.

C. H. Townsend Photographers took this photograph of Daisy White when she graduated from Willimantic Normal School. One of the schools she taught at was the Jones Street School, from 1920 to 1922. Her students included Frank and Mary Pizzitola; Jennie, Henrietta, and Joseph Sztaba (the family now spells it Staba); Bertha, Dorothy, and Harris Goldberg; Carrie, Mary, Josephine, and Stanley Zawisza; and Bertha Goldberg. This photograph is courtesy of the Ely collection.

The Gull Schoolhouse was located off Old Colchester Road in Amston. It was also called District Six. The school closed in 1919, but reopened in 1929. Henrietta Green began her teaching career there in 1930. Her class consisted of 15 children in grades one through eight. She and her husband obtained the school and moved it onto their property in 1970, where Henrietta frequently conducted tours and re-enactments for many children and adult visitors.

In 1935, students from the Hebron Center and Gilead Schools met at the Green for a joint photograph. This picture, from the Jones-Porter collection, shows 23 children. Gibson Porter is clearly recognizable on the far left in the center row, as is Olive White, fifth from the left in the center row. Others identified in the photograph are George Gonci, Frank Fishbone, Jeanne Ives, John Baron Sr., and Christine Pagach in the front row.

Henrietta Green was one of the most beloved and longest-tenured teachers in Hebron's one-room schoolhouses. She believed in maintaining Hebron's past, and preserved all of the old books and even student paintings from the Gull Schoolhouse. After Henrietta passed away, the town moved the Gull to the center of town, adjacent to the historic Hebron Records Building. Plans to restore the school as a museum are under way.

On the occasion of Hebron's bicentennial in 1908, the Hebron Center School (now the VFW/American Legion building) was gaily decorated with flags and banners. The schoolhouse continued in operation until 1949, when the new consolidated school was built. As Hebron approaches its tercentennial in 2008, one can only imagine the decorations and parades that will mark the celebration of 300 years of history.

Mertelle E. Goodwin was the Hebron Center School teacher throughout the 1920s. Her students included Arthur Keefe; Ed and Sophie Pomprowicz; Andrew and Richard Ives; John Horton; Clarence and Grace Rathbun; Julia and Mary Gonci; Mabel, Elsworth, and Howard Porter; Nancy Kulynyck; and Leo Kowalski. Mertelle married the superintendent, C. M. Larcomb, and retired from teaching until 1943, when she taught at the Jones Street School for one year.

Theresa Walsh was the Hebron Center School teacher in 1933. Earl Porter and Henry Pomprowicz are pictured on the left in the first row. Merle Jones is shown fourth from the left in the second row, sitting next to Alberta Hilding. Elsie Hills, Gordon Rathbun, and Bill Griffin are on the far right in the third row. Bradford Smith, Dorothy Gray, Mabel Hills, and Jane Pomprowicz stand on the far left in the fourth row.

In the third row up, Marie Smith stands to the left of Theresa Walsh (center), who taught grades five through eight at the Hebron Center School in 1936. The surnames of the students are all familiar names of longtime residents: Ives, Martin, Smith, Jones, Brehant, Gonci, Hills, Porter, Pomprowicz, Fickett, Griffin, Garlich, Gray, Wilson, and Kulynyck. Students identified in the front row are, from left to right, Helen Ives, Sylvia Martin, Merle Jones, Dorothy Brehant, Annie Gonci, and Helen Gonci.

This 1905 photograph depicts students in the Hebron Select School. Select school classes were conducted in the town hall for two years, after which students were transferred to Bacon Academy in Colchester to complete their education. Among the students seen here is Edward Smith (on the far right in the back row). This picture shows the seriousness of this young man who, between farming chores, would write volumes of poetry. Marie Smith Billard, Edward's daughter, still has his original, handwritten poems.

Edward A. Smith and his sister, Florence E. Smith, are shown in this August 1949 photograph from the Billard collection. After years of maintaining the Burrows Hill schoolhouse—believed to be the oldest schoolhouse in Hebron—the family did some restoration work, and opened it up for public tours on a limited basis. At the grand opening, Ed and Florence dressed in period clothing to greet the many visitors.

This 1936 photograph from the Billard collection shows the eighth-grade class at the Hebron School (now the American Legion). From left to right are the following: (first row) Carlton Jones, Merle Jones, and Dwight Martin; (second row) Marie Smith, Catherine Fickett, teacher Theresa Walsh, Elsie Garbich, and Elsie Hills. During World War II, 126 men and 2 women from Hebron served our country. Five of them died, including Carlton Porter Jones, who is pictured here with his classmates.

Six

THE PLACES

The Grange Hall stands at the junction of Gilead Street and Hall Road. Next to the old town hall, the Grange, built in 1905, was the second most important location for community events in the early 1900s. Abandoned in the 1950s, it has been restored as a private residence under two owners. The Grange has been featured in several publications (*Yankee Magazine*, *Home*, and *Connecticut Magazine*) that focused on the theme of converting a unique structure into a home. The current owners have added a pond, gazebo, and extensive gardens.

Previously known as the Rev. Samuel Peters House, this house eventually became the property of Gov. John Peters, and now is owned by the Hortons. Much history surrounds this property. Cesar Peters, who was a servant to Reverend Sam prior to Sam's flight to England during the Revolutionary War, continued to care for the property for years. Hebron residents rewarded Cesar's dedication in 1787, when they rescued his family from slave traders.

While sitting on the front porch of the Amston Inn, visitors could gaze out and see the Ams Mansion, probably one of the best-known homes in Hebron. Today, while the young trees shown in the background now obscure that same view, the house still stands in majestic glory, a tribute to the booming economy of its time.

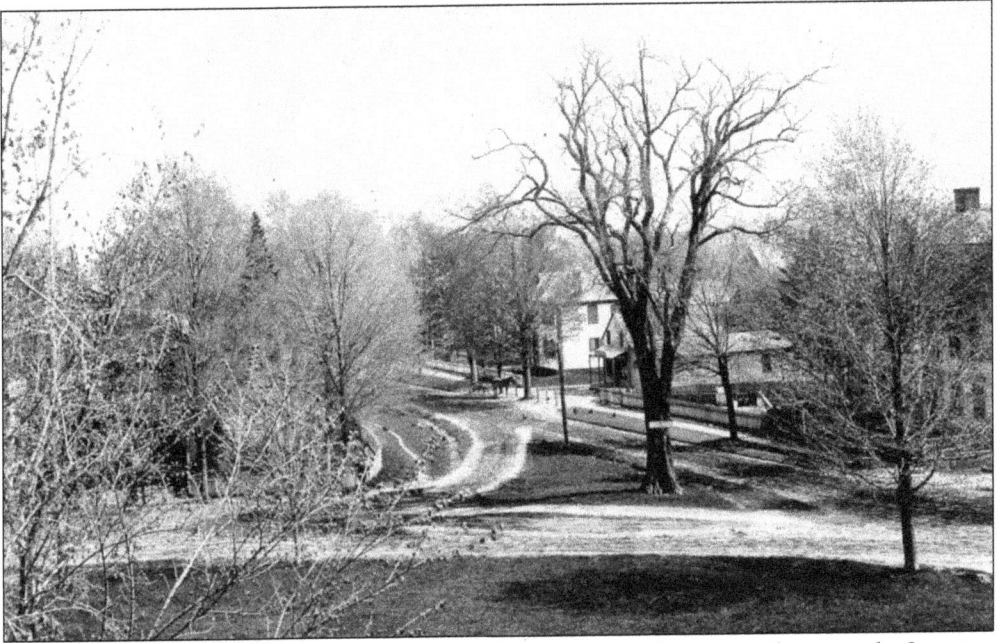

This famous photograph, taken c. 1890, has been reprinted on several postcards. Imagine standing on the roof of the First Congregational Church and looking south. The old elm that graced the town for centuries stands in the center; the Post store and house is on the right, though trees partially obscure the view. Notice the chickens searching for loose grain in front of the store.

Gilead Street is seen in a southward view from the Gilead Cemetery in 1941. The Lyman house is shown on the right in the foreground; in the background is the Hodge home. Just past the Hodges', but not visible in this photograph, was Fogil's store. Gilead Elementary School was eventually built on the left side of the road, across from Fogil's. The road was re-engineered to include a curve at the time of the school's construction.

The barn and shed on the Warner farm were built in 1724, making them some of the oldest structures in Gilead. The old homestead, pictured here in 1920 courtesy of the Raymond collection, was built in 1811, but burned down in 1935. A new house was promptly rebuilt on the same site by William Talcott Warner, and is currently occupied by Scott and Joan Warner.

In 1894, the Great Northern Survey Company of Albany, New York, went door to door in Hebron, offering to take property pictures for the grand sum of $1.50. The Woodworth family on Jones Street (close to today's intersection with Hope Valley Road) accepted the offer. The house was probably built in the early half of the 1700s; it was torn down in 1933. Pictured from left to right are George Thompson, David Carver, and Riley Woodworth.

According to land records, Ezekiel Jones, a descendent of one of the original Hebron settlers, built this home in 1773 to accommodate his growing brood of children (10 in all). The home remained in the Jones family until 1917; it was later sold to the Wrights, the Cafazzos, and finally, the Attardos. Stanley and Natalie Attardo Walas live in the house today.

John Graves built the Brown/Waldo home on Church Street, just south of the Green, between 1800 and 1830. The red brick used to build the structure is the same as that used for St. Peter's Episcopal Church and Governor Peters's home. The house is an excellent example of the Early Federal–style home. Today, it is the residence of Paul and Carla Pomprowicz.

Like many historic homes in Hebron, the Jared B. Tennant house on Wall Street, which dates back to the 1800s, fell prey to the demolition block. The house was taken down on August 7, 1974, per order of the Burritt Mutual Savings Bank. The bank is no longer in business.

The Footehills Farm on Gilead Street, pictured here in the early 1930s, was the home of generations of the Foote family. What is interesting about this photograph is the roof: notice the flat roof on the east side of the home (right side of the photograph). This was very rare in New England. When the flat roof blew off in the 1938 hurricane, it was replaced with the more traditional pitched roof.

Most residents will not recognize the landscape in this original photograph from the DeGray collection. The Caroline Kellogg (now Bogue) house is shown on the left, and the Fuller-Porter house (now Staff Mates) is shown in the center. The barn on the right was torn down when the state decided that Route 66 should go right through it.

No book on Hebron would be complete without a photograph of what was once known as "Shelter Rock" and is now called "Eagle Rock." In past years, the rock has been painted to resemble a frog, a whale, and a turtle. In 1989, former Regional Hebron Andover Marlborough High School student (and now New York artist) Jason Sawyer painted the rock to look like an eagle. Tara Graham of East Hampton assisted Sawyer in 2002 when he returned to give the rock a facelift with a new coat of paint.

It is hard to believe this is Gilead Street (Route 85) in 1907, looking north from the Gilead Congregational Church parsonage. The Way house on the right still stands. The Warner house on the left was destroyed by fire in 1935; however, the garage and shed of the Warner house survived. They may be the oldest structures in Gilead today.

This house, located just south of the Hebron center, is generally called the Pendleton house or "Pendletonia" because of the many years Dr. Cyrus Pendleton and his family lived there. The current owners, Robert and Paula Joan Pagach Toomey, have renamed it "Tara Mara." The house was built in 1816 by John Graves, and it is considered a fine example of the Federal architecture popular at that time.

The Fuller-Porter house has been the center of many social activities, almost since Hebron was incorporated in 1708. The original house, usually called "Fuller's Tavern," served as an inn and a local watering hole until it burned down in 1888. Horace Fuller Porter rebuilt the house in 1889. This picture is courtesy of the DeGray collection.

Hebron's old town hall is shown c. 1900. The structure was originally built as a Methodist church in 1838. The Methodists didn't stay long; they closed the doors in 1850, and sold the building to the town in 1863. It was not only the town hall, it was also the center of social life in Hebron for almost a century. The historical society now owns the building.

Prophet's Rock has features that offer shelter where a fire can be built. Legend has it that in 1706 two women set out to find their husbands. Night's darkness, along with the cry of wolves, forced the women to seek safety. They climbed up on the rock, and called out for their husbands; soon they were reunited. The rock is on property that was owned by the Smith family until recently and now belongs to the town.

The Caroline Kellogg house, built in 1790, is named after an early librarian at the Douglas Library. There is a central hallway running the full length of the square house, and a hip roof held in place by one central pin, which is still visible in the attic. During the days when Amos Bassett lived in the house, the first meeting of the Missionary Society in the United States was held in the front room.

Seven

THE MEMORIES

Many well-known residents are shown in this 1929 photograph of the Bert Lyman Band. Band members are, from left to right, as follows: (first row) Edward Foote, Dick Ives, David Porter, Bill Warner, Andrew Hooker, Stanley Keefe, unidentified boy, Harold Cummings, Howard Porter, and unidentified man; (second row) Bert Lyman, Herb Porter, Andy Ives, two unidentified boys, Jessie Hills, and Gordon Bevins; (third row) Merle Jones, Aceynath Jones, Marjorie Foote, unidentified boy, Sherwood Keefe, Norton Warner, John Hooker, Wendal Deeter, Everett Hutchinson, Leonard Porter, Edward Pomprowicz, and unidentified man.

Pictured here, from the Pomprowicz collection, is an original "union box." The outside of the box was carved, and the inside had velvet on the left to protect the daguerreotype on the right. The box is also called a footlocker. The man in the photograph is Lucius H. Jagger, brother of James Henry Jagger, and a Hebron resident who served in the Civil War. Lucius died in a Confederate prison in Beaufort, South Carolina, in 1864.

In this rare 1882 photograph, one clearly sees the devastation caused by the great fire. The Lord barn, shown in the background, was spared. The chimney of the Leonard Cash store is still standing. With most homes and businesses destroyed along the north side of what is now Route 66, John Sibun wrote, "Many of the people were financially ruined, and almost everyone was caught up in the gloom."

Hebron had its own Fife and Drum Corps well over 100 years ago. A. S. Coates sponsored these fellows (although here one sees more drums than fifes). According to John Sibun: "The Coateses had a well known drumming band, and no Hebron parade was complete without its presence in the late 19th century. The hills of Hope Valley vibrated daily to the uninhibited practice of Coates and close family friends."

Elegant handwriting on the back of this delightful photograph from the Pomprowicz collection notes that the picture was taken on July 4, 1899, at North Pond, Amston. The names of the young people gathered for the holiday events are unknown, yet the attire is revealing: all wore hats and ties or some other neckpiece. Notice that almost all of the hats have ribbon around them, which was typical of the period.

After their boating adventure at the lake, the July 4th celebrants moved on to the picnic. Picnics were among the most important community and family events in Hebron for decades. Betsy Foote Osborn remembers that the greatest incentive for finishing chores was the promise of a picnic at the end of a long day, made by her mother, Marion Walker Odell Foote, to her children Betsy, Mary Ann, Edward, and John.

This wonderful 1890 photograph prominently features Della Wilcox Porter in the center. Her husband, Roger, is second from the left. Others shown are Mary and George Mitchell, Bertha and Frank Little, Charles Hough, and Gertrude and Inez Porter. Inez was one of the first paid librarians at the Douglas Library (35 cents a day), and later married Arthur Gillette. Gertrude eventually married Hough; she was an original library trustee.

This never-before-seen "carte de visite," from the Pomprowicz collection, pictures a young doctor Charles Douglas c. 1890. Pre-dating the better-known calling cards of the early 1900s, the carte de visite was a popular fad in the late 1800s. The cartes were tiny, measuring a mere 3.25 inches by 1.75 inches. When making a social call, people would deposit their carte de visite in a bowl located in the entryway.

This wonderful photograph from the Pomprowicz collection, dated October 15, 1901, shows, from left to right, Herbert Wilcox, Charles Hough, and Will Sims standing, and Mary Devenport, Gertrude Porter, Inez Porter, Leslie Raymond, and May Bissell seated. The group was about to set off for the American Exhibition in Buffalo, New York. The excitement about the upcoming trip is evident on the faces of these young friends.

"The Citizens of the Town of Hebron, Conn., will celebrate the Bi-Centennial Anniversary of its incorporation the week commencing August 23, 1908." With these words, dignitaries throughout the state were invited to participate in a variety of activities, starting with church services on Sunday, and ending with a picnic on Thursday. Ida Porter Douglas was a major organizer of the event.

This famous 1908 postcard photograph of Hebron's bicentennial baseball team is intriguing. Cyrus E. Pendleton, a doctor (seen at the far right in the front row), was the son of Cyrus H. Pendleton, who also practiced medicine in Hebron. Frank Smith (second from the left in the back row) was the team's first African American player. Notice the motley assortment of uniforms: some have an "H," some say "Hebron," and one says "East Hampton."

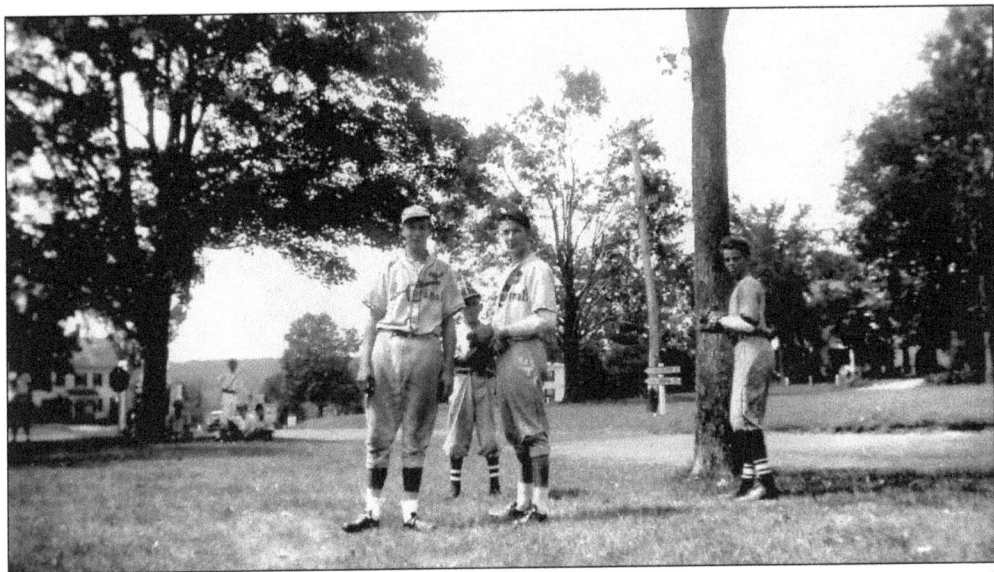

Life was great in 1915, and the Green was the center of all town life. On the back of this original photograph from the Pomprowicz collection, someone wrote, "The boys were practicing for a ball game so I snapped their picture." Featured from left to right are Sunny Griffin, Len Porter (in background), Horace Porter, and Frank Smith.

Many social events at the old town hall in the late 1800s included the Tennant family orchestra. The children of Frances and George Tennant were musically gifted on a variety of instruments. Charles Tennant Sr. moved his family to the Yukon around the turn of the century. In the front row, second from the left, is a rare view of Charles Tennant Jr., who died during the family's sojourn in Alaska.

People of all ages love to fish in all weather, and that passion is centuries old. In this photograph from the Pomprowicz collection, George Hills and George C. Tennant Sr. admire their catch after ice fishing on Amston Lake. The photograph was taken *c.* 1910. Notice that even in the simple task of fishing, hats and topcoats were worn, representative of the importance of one's dress in that era.

Children love horses, and this 1915 photograph from the Pomprowicz collection clearly demonstrates that. Pictured from left to right are Dorothy Tennant, Clarissa Lord, Helen Hough, and Mildred Hough. In the background is the Hebron Congregational Church. Helen Hough later became famous as an actress in local plays, both in Hebron and in surrounding communities.

Few modern-day Hebron residents would be able to recognize the road in this photograph as the original Church Street. Prior to 1927, when the paved street was put in, cattle and other livestock had been moved up and down Church Street on a frequent basis for generations. Almost all homes had fences in front of them to keep errant cows out of the gardens; some of those original fences still stand today.

To put in the paved road ultimately designated as Route 85, the state of Connecticut took down three rows of centuries-old trees along Church Street in 1927. This photograph shows tree trunks that lined the road for months prior to the street being paved. The Hilding home (now the parsonage for Church of the Holy Family) is shown to the left in the background. The typical Model T Ford is shown on the right.

By late 1908, Hebron's baseball team had gained renown, and the change in uniforms is noticeable. The shirts and pants match. Cyrus E. Pendleton was still playing (seen third from the left in the back row). The gentleman with the dark suit and bow tie (in the center of the back row) is Chester Tennant, brother of photographer H. F. Tennant. The other gentleman in a suit is Fred Rathbun. This picture was reproduced on numerous postcards.

This is a fun sign that appeared in Hebron in the early 1900s before the Church Street/Route 85 road was put in. It was probably meant for the automobiles that were appearing more and more on the dirt road, but local residents laughed knowing that livestock were the most frequent users of Church Street.

The Smith family of Burrows Hill Road was quite active in local plays performed at the old town hall and the Hebron Grange. Seen in this 1920 photograph are Smith siblings Florence (far left), Edward (second from left), and Eugene (far right), along with Eugene's wife, Elizabeth Rathbun. They are dressed in costume while preparing for one of their performances. Florence was a school principal for many years, and the Florence E. Smith School of Science, Math & Technology in West Hartford was named in her honor.

Residents have heard about the famous auctions of the early 1900s that were routinely held on Friday nights. This photograph, from the Robinson collection, depicts the many automobiles gathered in the center of town in 1916. The Horton house is featured in the center of the photograph, with the Hebron Records Building slightly to the right. Residents bid on anything from cattle to collectibles. More than anything, the auction was a social event.

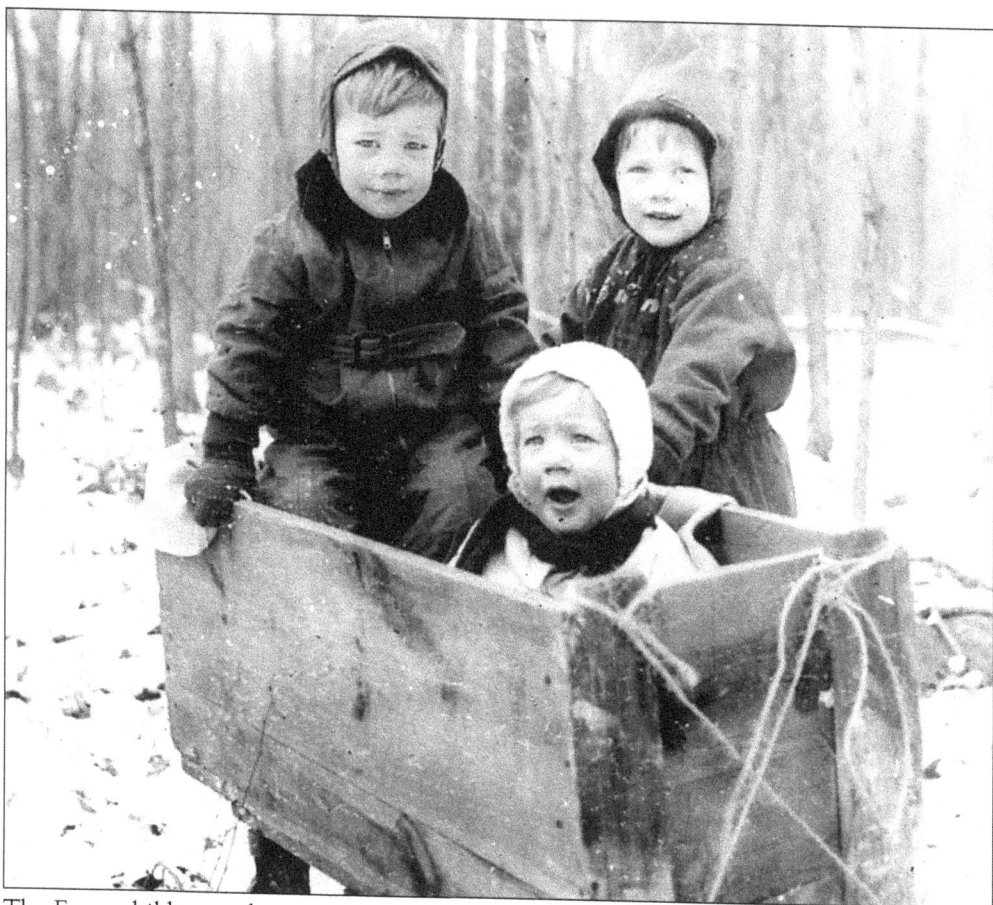

The Foote children, as have most Hebron children through the generations, enjoyed sledding whenever there was enough snow. Pictured from left to right are John, Mary Ann, and Debby Foote. The sled was one of the old flexible flyers—it was really just an old crate in which machinery parts had been shipped. The kids' father, Ed Foote, simply roped the crate to a sled. Yankee ingenuity at its best.

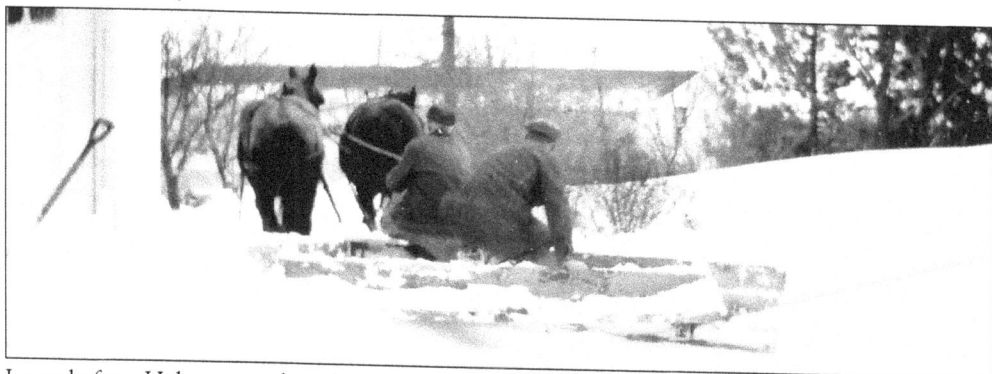

Long before Hebron purchased its bright orange snowplows, local farmers took care of the problem in their own way: with horses and a homemade contraption. This 1939 photograph, from the Hilding collection, shows brothers Ed and Sam Hilding setting off from their farm on Church Street to clear the roads and paths to the barn. Sam provides the weight to keep the plow close to the ground.

George Merle Jones is shown here in 1917 with his childhood friend, Robert Porter, on the town green. Merle is leaning on a gun; Rob, who joined the army a year later, is holding an American flag. American Legion Post No. 95 is named for Jones and Arthur Keefe, who died serving their country in World Wars I and II, respectively. Porter's sons, Gibson and Milton, served in World War II.

Merle Jones was home on leave when this last photograph of him, from the Ous collection, was taken August 25, 1918. The difference in his appearance from the 1917 photograph with Rob Porter (at top of page) is haunting. The Green is still seen in the background, where Merle had happily played baseball throughout his youth. He died in Georgia of typhoid fever at age 22 on October 2, 1918.

Hebron's resident blacksmith, Frederick John Brehant, was the personal blacksmith and groomsman to Gen. John "Black Jack" Pershing, commander of American forces in Europe in World War I. This photograph, from the Brehant collection, was taken in France in 1918. Brehant's daughter Dorothy Taggart remembers that few had the much-needed skills to keep the horses shoed and ready for battle. Frederick Brehant fought in five major battles in the war.

Frederick John Brehant is shown here in uniform. The Brehant brothers had relocated their blacksmith shop from the north side to Amston in 1915. Brehant, who was not yet an American citizen, went off to war shortly thereafter. When he returned, the brothers continued to shoe horses, but their blacksmith shop was better known as the only one to shoe oxen in the area.

This image from the Pomprowicz collection shows the intersection of what is today Route 66 and Route 85. At the time of this photograph, a board announcing important community events stood at the intersection. While it's difficult to read, the community board here was announcing a war rally as the United States entered World War I. In the foreground, a passerby contemplates the future at this momentous time in history.

Daniel G. Horton lovingly holds his nephew John E. Horton, in this photograph from the Horton collection. Daniel was leaving for service in World War I. He is standing in front of the Governor Peters house; the Tennant house is shown in the left background. This is a wonderful southward view of Church Street as it was in 1917. Many hitching posts are stationed along the road.

It was Memorial Day 1922. With World War I over, people celebrated the heroes of the past, with firm hope that young men and women would not be called again to serve in far-off places. The Hortons decorated their old truck, which is seen here parked in front of Pendletonia, the former home of local doctor Cyrus Pendleton. It is now the Toomey home.

The Barnstormers were a popular square-dancing band in the 1930s and 1940s, which featured Gilead residents Norton Warner (far right), Bill Warner (second from right), and Andy Hooker (third from right). The band members loaded up their equipment into an old hay truck every Friday night and performed throughout the northeastern part of Connecticut. In 1939, the Barnstormers branched out and played at the World's Fair in New York.

Depicted here is first selectman Claude Jones's copy of the Hebron annual town report for the fiscal year 1922–1923. The town's budget that year was $35,400.07; W. S. Hewitt was town treasurer. The report is a detailed record of the town's activities. Everything is documented, including the names of all those in town who had registered dogs, and even a payment of $4.50 to Deems Buell "for services as auditor."

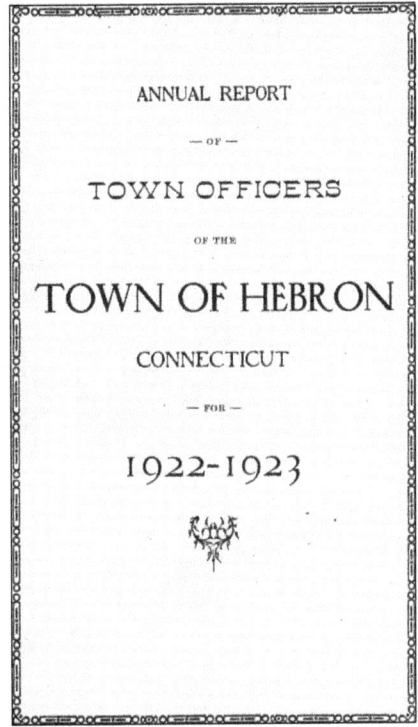

ANNUAL REPORT

— OF —

TOWN OFFICERS

OF THE

TOWN OF HEBRON

CONNECTICUT

— FOR —

1922-1923

Gilead mothers and their children decided to take a field trip into town in 1926. On the steps of Hebron's old town hall, they posed for this photograph of the big day. Several of the children were obviously excited; notice that a few faces are blurred because the children were moving around so much.

This is the original Hebron fire station, built in the late 1930s. In the top photograph showing the building under construction, Gladys Miner's house is seen in the background. The completed project is shown in the bottom photograph. The firehouse's site was just in front of the current Hebron Fire House Company No. 1 on Main Street. The building itself was moved in 1980 to its current location on Pendleton Drive. It is now the home of Datatype.

In 1937, Hebron got its very first fire truck. After years of losing buildings and fighting fires with buckets of water, it was a welcome acquisition. Hebron Volunteer Fire Department members are now restoring this same fire truck. They hope to complete the restoration and be able to display it as a reminder of a proud moment in Hebron's history.

Residents gathered at the old Amston Inn on south Church Street in order to see a demonstration of the fire department's new equipment. Carlton Jones was the fire chief. This view shows the residents gathered for the event, looking toward the Ams Mansion. According to the Horton family, there was no fire at the inn; the firefighters were just testing the new equipment.

This rare photograph from the Jones-Porter collection depicts Gordon Earl Porter and Merle Natalie Jones in 1931. The children had just performed together in a play at St. Peter's Church summer school. Always friends, Merle and Earl were married in 1946 after he returned from the war. They had three daughters—Gayle, Patricia, and Kimberly. Goats and donkeys still peacefully graze in the front yard of the Porter's homestead.

Connecticut witnessed "the perfect storm" in 1938. It was a devastating hurricane that damaged almost every property in Hebron. Damage to the Griffing's house on Wall Street is shown in this photograph from the Hilding collection. The entire side of the house was blown off, in addition to massive tree uprooting. Seen on the left is the remainder of the shed, which was blown apart and pushed into the house.

Little in Hebron escaped the 1938 hurricane. This photograph, also from the Hilding collection, was taken in the center of town, looking at the Hebron Records Building (on the right) and the Horton house (at the far left). Many of the largest trees in Hebron, which had been in existence since the town's incorporation in 1708, were lost forever.

The hurricane of 1938 didn't just uproot trees and crops. It also destroyed barns and farm equipment, thereby interrupting the primary economy. Thankfully, there was no loss of life. Pictured here, after the storm, is the Jones barn on Wall Street; the barn had been sold to Walt Doubleday just months before the hurricane. The Hilding family farm records and pictures serve as an excellent source for documenting this historic event.

This 1938 photograph of Lillian Griffing (left) and Merle Jones, taken in front of Charles Hilding's home on Church Street (now the Houston home), is famous. The hurricane's devastation takes on new perspective. Jones, an athlete and avid softball player all her life, had earned her letter sweater from Windham High School during her sophomore year for basketball. It says 1940 because that was her anticipated year of graduation.

The hurricane tore the roof completely off the Brehant barn, did minor damage to the roof of the house, and uprooted many trees in the family's orchards. In later years, reflecting on the damage done to her family homestead, Dorothy Brehant Taggart wrote, "No, lover of that ancient Russet apple tree, it was not I who willed that she should end in such a hard and absolute demise."

The Ladies Aid Society of the Congregational church is pictured here in the 1930s. The organization was later called Women's Fellowship. Some of the members shown are Ruth Ellis Young, Winifred Ellis, Lida Way, Clara Ellis, Edith Ellis Bragg, Mabel Warner, Annie Smith, and Emily Ellis. The Ellis women were actively involved in the organization.

Viola Porter took this photograph (from the DeGray collection) of daughters Virginia and Roberta, with their faithful dog Prince, in December 1942. It was an unusual winter, and on this particular day the temperature was 15 degrees below zero. The weather led Edward Smith to write his poem "Sub-Zero": "They say in plain English and speak out real bold. They don't like this weather; it's too darned cold!"

The happiness of the newly engaged Marie Purington Smith and Alfred Barnes Billard is clearly evident in this photograph; they were married in 1943. Marie and Al had four sons: Roger Alan (born 1946), Thomas Paul (born 1948), Peter James (born 1950), and David Michael (born 1955). They remain a close-knit family, as well as neighbors on Burrows Hill Road.

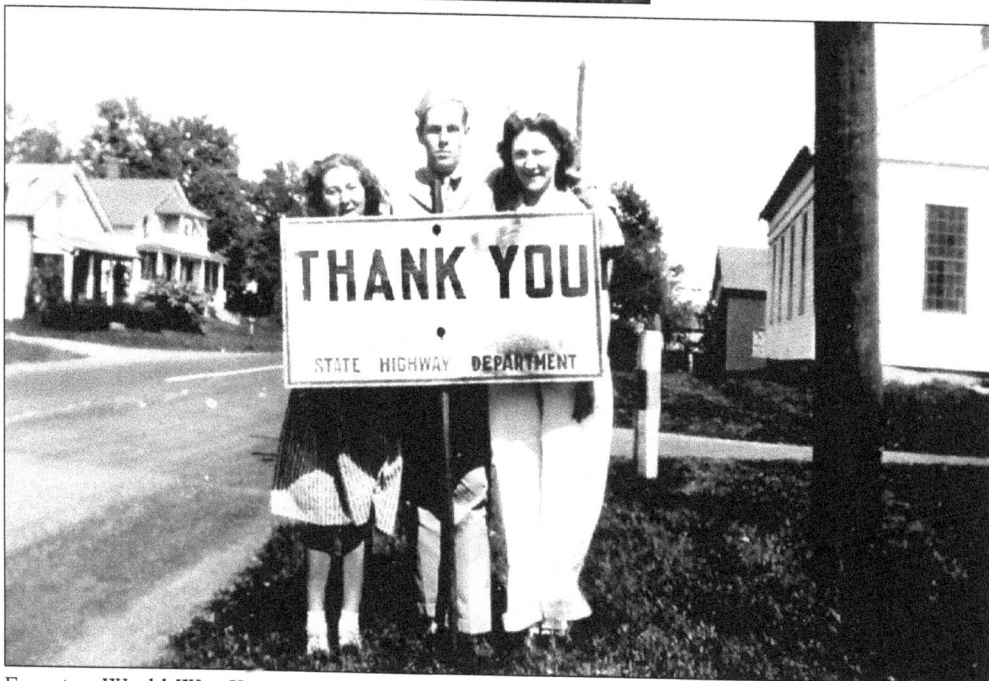

Entering World War II was not an easy time for Hebron residents. This photograph, taken in 1942, depicts Josie Pomprowicz, Charles Johnston, and Virginia Johnston with a state highway sign that simply says "Thank You." The old town hall is shown in the background on the right.

In September 1942, all Hebron residents received this postcard inviting them to bid farewell to the great cannon. Residents were also encouraged to bring their own metal scrap to aid the war effort, and to contribute other items (such as vegetables) for the Red Cross. As always in the tight-knit community, an auction of valuable items and a parade capped the occasion.

SALE & FAREWELL

Saturday, Sept. 5, at Hebron Green

On this day G. Merle Jones Post, American Legion No. 95, will turn its trophy cannon—our Symbol of Victory in 1918—back into the battle with Full Military Honors.

GET OUT YOUR OLD METALS !

Send word to Salvage Chairman, I. C. Turshen. The trucks will call at your house and fall in behind the cannon for its Great Send-off.

**THIS IS MORE THAN A DEMONSTRATION !
IT WILL SEND TEN TO TWENTY TONS
OF IRON AND STEEL INTO THE
BATTLE FOR FREEDOM !**

DAY'S EVENTS

**11:30 to 1:30 BOOT AND BARTER FOR
THE RED CROSS**

If you have something—a good overcoat, a pitcher and washbowl, an armful of vegetables, a good frying-pan—bring it in and find a person to trade with. But there must be some boot—all the boot goes to the Red Cross.

12:00 to 1:00 FOOD SALE AND LUNCH

1:30 *AUCTION.* C. B. Jones will auction off 27 valuable donated articles—fur coat, mystery boxes, chair swing, etc.

3:00 GRAND FINALE   ORDER OF PARADE

The Colors, Legion and Honor Guard, Drum Corps, Hebron Defense Council and Citizens, The Cannon, and Truck-loads of Scrap.

**HELP SAY FAREWELL TO OUR CANNON--
AND HITLER !**

Shown in this image from the Gray collection is the great cannon, a relic and reminder of World War I that had graced the Green for many years. The cannon was located across from the Hebron Records Building. The Horton house is visible in the background.

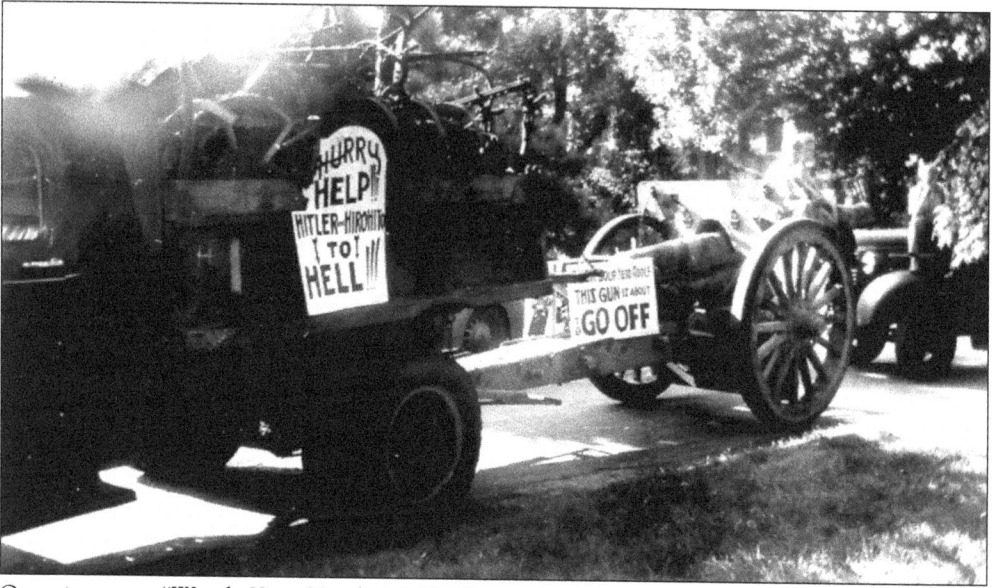

One sign says: "Watch Your Head Adolf! This gun is about to Go Off." Residents gathered in front of the G. Merle Jones American Legion Post No. 95 to send off the great cannon to be melted down. The date was September 5, 1942. The war did not end until 1945, after five Hebron men had lost their lives. Ira Turshen drove the streets of Hebron, asking residents for metal donations for the war effort.

Irving Griffin, in his U.S. Air Force uniform, smiles broadly in this 1942 photograph. Griffin was admired for his athletic skills, and was particularly famous for his abilities in ice hockey. The Griffin children grew up in a house located behind old town hall; the house no longer stands. Griffin, described as a free spirit by his childhood friends, was also known to attend all the square dances in the area.

This never-before-seen photograph from the Ely collection depicts Arthur Keefe, son of Maurice Keefe, standing against the backdrop of Amston Lake in 1935. Keefe was one of the five young Hebron men killed in World War II. Edward Smith wrote, "I don't suppose you realize, and yet I'm sure you know, that Hebron is quite different than it was a week ago."

Arthur M. Keefe was the first Hebron serviceman to lose his life in World War II. He was fighting in Sicily with the army when he was killed on July 11, 1943. This photograph, also from the Ely collection, is believed to be the last photograph taken of him prior to his death.

Joseph Kowalski was a sergeant in the army during World War II. He received a Purple Heart when he was wounded in the Battle of the Bulge, where more than one million men fought in the month-long battle in 1944. Kowalski, born in 1918, grew up on Wellswood Road, and was a popular pitcher on the Hebron baseball team for many years. His sister, Eleanor Wengrzynek, still resides in Amston.

This unusual photograph depicts Edward (left) and Henry Pomprowicz, who served in the U.S. Navy during World War II. At that time, artists would take a photograph, and then brush it up to make it look like a portrait. After the war, the brothers returned to Hebron. Ed served as a state representative; Henry ran a chicken farm off Hillcrest Drive in Amston, and later was the Amston postmaster in the early 1960s.

This photograph of Marshall Porter was taken in 1943. Porter had graduated from the Sioux Falls Radio and Mechanical School. Lucille Porter Jones wrote, in her *Destination Unknown*, "Yet visions of the future, the days must surely bring. Their mission? Ask each of the crew: 'To make our Freedom Ring.'" Attached to the poem was a note: "To Marshall, as he left to fly the Atlantic for an unknown destination."

This 1944 photograph from the Ous collection depicts a happy Marshall Porter. By then, he had flown more than 30 missions in his B-26, and was highly regarded as a radio operator. Marshall's plane was shot down shortly after this photograph was taken; he is officially missing in action. The family is not sure if his plane went down over France or the English Channel.

In her poem to Lloyd Gray, "To Lloyd: Happy Landings Gray Eagle," Lucille Jones wrote in 1944: "With wide spread wings and motors roaring, Came a war bird swiftly soaring. Dipped and nearly touched the tree tops, Greeted us by dipping lower, Thrilled us all by mighty power, Waved to us by way of greeting, Tipped a wing in lieu of meeting, Gave us all a farewell message, Started on an ocean passage . . ."

Rev. George MacLean Milne, shown here in 1943 with his wife, Janet Odell Milne, took a leave of absence from his duties as pastor for both Congregational churches in order to serve in the U.S. Navy during World War II. The photograph was taken on the steps of the Gilead Congregational Church just before Milne left for active duty as a chaplain, a position he held until 1946.

"The joy with which Mr. and Mrs. Raymond H. Jones received the news of V-E Day was abruptly and tragically shattered in the afternoon when they received a telegram from the War Department that their only son, Corporal Raymond Wilfred Jones, had been killed in action in Germany on April 26, 1945." — *Middletown Press*. Germany surrendered less than two weeks later on May 7, 1945, and Victory in Europe Day was declared May 8. Jones was only 20 years old.

Henry Jones (left), G. Earl Porter (center), and Lloyd Gray, on leave in 1944, posed for Gray's mother, Susan Miner Gray, who took this photograph in the driveway of their home next to the Hewitt house on the Green. Jones was a U.S. Navy aviation machinist; Porter was a corporal with the U.S. Marine Corps (and received a Purple Heart for wounds suffered on Iwo Jima); and Gray was a lieutenant in the U.S. Army Air Corps.

Gibson "Gib" Clinton Porter (left) and his brother Milton Robert are shown in this photograph dated April 23, 1944, from the DeGray collection. Gib received a Bronze Star in World War II; Milton today remains very active in the Hebron Veterans of Foreign Wars. They are the sons of Robert Fuller Porter and Viola Preston Porter.

Carlton Porter Jones was a stellar athlete and baseball player. At lower right, notice his handwritten note: "Love to all, Carlton." He was killed in action in France in 1944. His mother's heartbreak is felt in *Reflections*, a collection of Lucille Porter Jones's poetry: "Let the war be over quickly; Dear God—Send him home to me." And then: "Yet when we come to count the cost. Altho' we've won—So much we've lost."

4

375656 CC

UNITED STATES OF AMERICA
OFFICE OF PRICE ADMINISTRATION

WAR RATION BOOK FOUR

Issued to _Gordon Earl Porter_

(Print first, middle, and last names)

Complete address

Hebron Conn

READ BEFORE SIGNING

In accepting this book, I recognize that it remains the property of the United States Government. I will use it only in the manner and for the purposes authorized by the Office of Price Administration.

Void if Altered _Gordon Earl Porter_

(Signature)

It is a criminal offense to violate rationing regulations.

OPA Form R-145

16—35570-1

Many remember the ration coupons issued during World War II. Pictured above and below, courtesy of the Jones-Porter collection, are the original coupon books issued to G. Earl Porter and Merle N. Jones. Earl's has the official stamp of the "Hebron War Price & Rationing Board, Hebron, Conn." The U.S. Office of Price Administration reminded everyone, via a message on the back cover, not to try to buy sugar, coffee, gasoline, and other rationed goods without a coupon. The importance of salvaging tin cans was a message heard frequently; the metal was needed for the war effort.

NEVER BUY RATIONED GOODS

WITHOUT RATION STAMPS

NEVER PAY MORE THAN THE LEGAL PRICE

United States Office of Price Administration

IMPORTANT: When you have used your ration, salvage the TIN CANS and WASTE FATS. They are needed to make munitions for our fighting men. Cooperate with your local Salvage Committee.

4

CA

UNITED STATES OF AMERICA
OFFICE OF PRICE ADMINISTRATION

WAR RATION BOOK FOUR

Issued to _Merle N. Jones_

(Print first, middle, and last names)

Complete address _Hebron, Conn_

READ BEFORE SIGNING

In accepting this book, I recognize that it remains the property of the United States Government. I will use it only in the manner and for the purposes authorized by the Office of Price Administration.

Void if Altered _Merle N. Jones_

(Signature)

It is a criminal offense to violate rationing regulations.

OPA Form R-145

12—35570-1

This is a rare photograph of Joseph Gearhart, a Hebron resident killed at the Battle of Iwo Jima in World War II. Here, Gearhart, in uniform, gazes adoringly at his daughter, Miriam. Gearhart served with the U.S. Marines; 6,825 Marines were killed at the Battle of Iwo Jima—that is, one out of three servicemen sent to battle on that momentous day.

There was reason to celebrate the Memorial Day parade of 1949. Girl Scouts in uniform showed up in droves, carrying flowers for veterans. Members of the VFW are shown in the background, next to the Hebron Library. Bobby Kowalski, seen in the hooded jacket on the right, was watching his Uncle Joseph, who had returned home from the European theater.

The townspeople celebrated all day on the Green that Memorial Day. The war was over, the soldiers—men and women—were home. The joy is evident on the children's faces. One more time, families hoped to never have to send their children off to war again.

People tried to get back into the daily routine after the war; this postcard went out to residents reminding them of Old Home Day on August 20, 1949. As usual, many activities were planned. These Old Home Day events are thought to be the precursors to the Hebron Harvest Fair, now one of the largest in Connecticut.

OLD HOME DAY IN HEBRON

Recall the Past, Salute the Future

Visit 200 year Burrows Hill School

Dedicate Modern Consolidated School

AUGUST 20, 1949

BE HERE FOR

The Doll Carriage Parade and
    Baby Show,   10 A. M.
The Old-time Country Auction, 11 A.M.
The Ox-pulling Contest,   2 P. M.
    3 Classes of Competition
Tour of Hebron's Oldest School, 4 P. M.
Exhibits Old & New, from Far
    and Near,   12-6 P. M.
Dedication of the New School 7:30 P.M.

Dance on the Village Green, 9 P. M.

Clam Chowder Served all Day

HOME-COOKED FOOD FOR SALE

Hot Dogs, Ice Cream, Cookies, Etc.

Come & Spend the Day

This photograph, from the Jones-Porter collection, shows Claude Jones receiving a ribbon for his oxen team, Tom and Jerry, at the Connecticut State Fair. The son of Carlton Blish Jones and Ellen Hills Jones, Claude held many statewide positions, including state legislator and commissioner on domestic animals from 1940 to 1944. He died in 1949 when he fell while pitching hay to the cows being shown at the Danbury State Fair.

This photograph of a community picnic in 1949 is loaded with Cranick, Billard, Nygren, Foote, Ellis, Rathbun, Belden, Pixton, Taylor, Coolidge, Horton, Smith, and TenEyke families, all obviously enjoying themselves.

Prior to the advent of mechanical balers, hay was loosely collected and stored in the hay mows. To avoid losing the load of hay, it had to be placed and packed by a person on the truck. Here, that responsibility is handled by Marion Odell Foote, newly married and fresh out of suburban Westchester County, New York.

124

Alma Lever Porter, pictured here in 1941, was the longest-serving postmaster in Hebron history. For 33 years, from 1925 until 1958, she not only ran the post office, but she also sold ice cream, bread, and essentials in her little store located inside the building, along with Tydol gasoline out front. Porter was extremely active on the library committee. All four of her sons served in World War II.

This unusual photograph was taken in 1943, and features the Hebron Center School on the top and the children who attended it that year on the bottom. Teacher Henrietta Green is shown in the center of the third row. Children from grades one through eight attended the school.

250th Anniversary
OF THE
Town of Hebron, Connecticut

1708   HEBRON
CON.   1958

You are cordially invited to attend the
TWO HUNDRED FIFTIETH ANNIVERSARY
of the
TOWN OF HEBRON
Friday, Saturday and Sunday, July 18th, 19th, 20th, 1958
Friday Evening - Pageant
Saturday - Old Home Day and Parade
Sunday - Church Services
Tours to places of historical interest on
Saturday and Sunday.
Come, bring your family, and renew old acquaintances
Visit the home of your ancestors.

In July 1958, Hebron celebrated the 250th anniversary of its incorporation. Postcards announcing the event went out to everyone, including state dignitaries. Residents gaily decorated their homes, as seen below in the photograph of the Hough house on Marjorie Circle. The theme of the anniversary was patriotic, as well as celebratory. People were reminded not to forget the church services on Sunday.

Henrietta Green, a fervent preserver of Hebron history, is shown here in 1990 on the occasion of her 80th birthday. Her beloved dog, Mitzi, shares her lap. Many children wrote letters to Henrietta on this occasion, thanking her for her dedication to Hebron. Her contributions to the schools, the town, and the Hebron Historical Society will never be forgotten.

www.ingramcontent.com/pod-product-compliance
Lightning Source LLC
Chambersburg PA
CBHW050631110426
42813CB00007B/1781